200 Light
sugar-free recipes

hamlyn | **all color cookbook**

200 Light
sugar-free recipes

An Hachette UK Company
www.hachette.co.uk

First published in Great Britain in 2015 by
Hamlyn, a division of Octopus Publishing Group Ltd
Carmelite House, 50 Victoria Embankment
London EC4Y 0DZ
www.octopusbooks.co.uk

Distributed in the US by Hachette Book Group
1290 Avenue of the Americas, 4th and 5th Floors
New York, NY 10020

Distributed in Canada by Canadian Manda Group
664 Annette St., Toronto, Ontario, Canada M6S 2C8

Recipes in this book have previously appeared in other books
published by Hamlyn.

ISBN 978-0-600-63246-7

Printed and bound in China

2 3 4 5 6 7 8 9 10

Standard level kitchen spoon and cup measurements are used
in all recipes.

Ovens should be preheated to the specific temperature; if using a
convection oven, follow manufacturer's instructions for adjusting the
time and the temperature.

Eggs should be large unless otherwise stated. The U.S. Food and
Drug Administration advises that eggs should not be consumed raw.
This book contains dishes made with raw or lightly cooked eggs. It
is prudent for more vulnerable people, such as pregnant and nursing
mothers, people with weakened immune systems, the elderly,
babies, and young children, to avoid uncooked or lightly cooked
dishes made with eggs. Once prepared, these dishes should be kept
refrigerated and used promptly.

Milk should be whole unless otherwise stated.

Fresh herbs should be used unless otherwise stated. If unavailable,
use dried herbs as an alternative, but use one-third of the
quantities stated.

Pepper should be freshly ground black pepper unless
otherwise stated.

This book includes dishes made with nuts and nut derivatives.
It is advisable for customers with known allergic reactions to nuts
and nut derivatives and those who may be potentially vulnerable
to these allergies, such as pregnant and nursing mothers, people
with weakened immune systems, the elderly, babies, and children,
to avoid dishes made with nuts and nut oils. It is also prudent to
check the labels of prepared ingredients for the possible inclusion
of nut derivatives.

contents

introduction

introduction

this series

The Hamlyn All Color Light Series is a collection of books in a handy size, each filled with more than 200 healthy recipes on a variety of topics and cuisines to suit your needs.

The books are designed to help those people who are trying to lose weight by offering a range of delicious recipes that are low in calories but still high in flavor. The recipes shows the calorie count per portion, so you will know exactly what you are eating. These are recipes for real and delicious food, not ultra-dieting meals, so they will help you maintain your new, healthier eating plan for life. They must be used as part of a balanced diet, with the cakes and sweet dishes eaten only as an occasional treat.

how to use this book

All the recipes in this book are clearly marked with the number of calories (cal) per serving. The chapters cover different calorie bands: less than 500 calories, less than 400 calories, less than 300 calories, etc.

There are variations of each recipe at the bottom of the page. You should always check the calorie count, because they do vary and the calories in the variations can sometimes be more than in the original recipe.

The figures assume that you are using lean meat, so make sure you trim meat of all visible fat and remove the skin from chicken breasts. Use moderate amounts of oil and butter for cooking or low-fat/low-calorie alternatives (see page 13).

Don't forget to take note of the number of servings each recipe makes and divide up the quantity of food accordingly, so that you know exactly how many calories you are consuming. Be careful about side dishes and accompaniments, because they will add to the calorie content.

Above all, enjoy trying out the new flavors and exciting recipes that this book contains. Instead of dwelling on the thought that you are denying yourself your usual unhealthy snacks and treats, think of your new diet plan as a positive step toward a new and improved you. Not only will you lose weight and feel more confident, but your health

will benefit, the condition of your hair and nails will improve, and your skin will take on a healthy glow.

the risks of obesity

Up to half of women and two-thirds of men are overweight or obese in the developed world today. Being overweight not only can make us unhappy with our appearance, but can also lead to serious health problems, including heart disease, high blood pressure, and diabetes. When someone is obese, it means they are overweight to the point that it could start to seriously threaten their health. In fact, obesity ranks as a close second to smoking as a possible cause of cancer. Obese women usually have more complications during and after pregnancy, and people who are overweight or obese are also more at risk of developing coronary heart disease, gallstones, osteoarthritis, high blood pressure, and type 2 diabetes.

how can I tell if I am overweight?

The best way to tell if you are overweight is to work out your body mass index (BMI). To do so, divide your weight in pounds by your height in inches squared and multiply by 703. (For example, if you are 5 feet 6 inches and weigh 146 pounds, the calculation is: 5 x 12 = 60, then 60 + 6 = 66 inches; 66 x 66 = 4,356; 146 ÷ 4,356 = 0.0335; 0.0335 x 703 = 23.56. (Or use an online BMI calculator.) Compare the figure to the list below (the figures apply to only healthy adults).

less than 20	underweight
20–25	healthy
25–30	overweight
Over 30	obese

As we all know by now, one of the major causes of obesity is eating too many calories.

what is a calorie?

Our bodies need energy to stay alive, grow, keep warm, and be active. We get the energy we need to survive from the food and drinks we consume—more specifically, from the fat, carbohydrate, protein, and alcohol that they contain.

A calorie (cal), as anyone who has ever been on a diet will know, is the unit used

to measure how much energy different foods contain. A calorie can be scientifically defined as the energy required to raise the temperature of 1 gram of water from 58°F to 60°F. A kilocalorie (kcal) is 1,000 calories and—although we call them calories—it is, in fact, kilocalories that we usually mean when we talk about the calories in different foods.

Different food types contain different numbers of calories. For example, a gram of carbohydrate (starch or sugar) provides 3.75 calories, protein provides 4 calories per gram, fat provides 9 calories per gram, and alcohol provides 7 calories per gram. So, fat is the most concentrated source of energy—weight for weight, it provides just over twice as many calories as either protein or carbohydrate—with alcohol not far behind. The energy content of a food or drink depends on how many grams of carbohydrate, fat, protein, and alcohol are present.

how many calories do we need?

The number of calories we need to consume varies from person to person, but your body weight is a clear indication of whether you are eating the right amount. Body weight is simply determined by the number of calories you are eating compared to the number of calories your body is using to maintain itself and needed for physical activity. If you regularly consume more calories than you use, you will start to gain weight as extra energy is stored in the body as fat.

Based on our relatively inactive modern-day lifestyles, most nutritionists recommend that women should aim to consume about 2,000 calories per day, and men an amount of about 2,500 calories. Of course, the amount of energy required depends on your level of activity; the more active you are, the more energy you need to maintain a stable weight.

a healthier lifestyle

To maintain a healthy body weight, we usually need to expend as much energy as we consume; to lose weight, therefore, energy expenditure must exceed intake of calories. So, exercise is an important tool in the fight to lose weight.

Physical activity doesn't just help us control body weight; it also helps to reduce our appetite and is known to have beneficial

10 minutes are equally beneficial. Children and young people should be encouraged to get at least 60 minutes of moderate-intensity exercise every day.

Some activities will use more energy than others. The following list shows some examples of the energy a person weighing 132 pounds would expend doing the following activities for 30 minutes:

activity	energy
Ironing	69 calories
Cleaning	75 calories
Walking	99 calories
Golf	129 calories
Fast walking	150 calories
Cycling	180 calories
Aerobics	195 calories
Swimming	195 calories
Running	300 calories
Sprinting	405 calories

make changes for life

The best way to lose weight is to try to adopt healthier eating habits that you can easily maintain all the time, not just when you are trying to lose weight. Aim to lose no more than 2 pounds per week to be sure that you lose only your fat stores. People who go on crash diets lose lean muscle as well as fat and are much more at risk of putting weight back on again soon afterward.

For a woman, the aim is to reduce her daily calorie intake to about 1,500 calories while she is trying to lose weight, then to settle

effects on the heart and blood that help prevent cardiovascular disease.

Many of us claim we don't enjoy exercise and simply don't have the time to fit it into our hectic schedules, so the easiest way to increase physical activity is by incorporating it into our daily routines, perhaps by walking or cycling instead of driving (particularly for short journeys), getting involved in more active hobbies, such as gardening, and taking small and simple steps, such as using the stairs instead of the elevator whenever possible.

As a general guide, adults should aim to participate in at least 30 minutes of moderate-intensity exercise, such as a brisk walk, five times a week. The 30 minutes does not have to occur all at once; three sessions of on about 2,000 calories per day thereafter to maintain her new body weight. Regular exercise will also make a huge difference.

improve your diet

For most of us, simply adopting a more balanced diet will reduce our calorie intake and lead to weight loss. Follow these simple recommendations:

- Eat more starchy foods, such as bread, potatoes, rice, and pasta. Assuming these replace the fattier foods you usually eat, and you don't smother them with oil or butter, this will help reduce the amount

of fat and increase the amount of fiber in your diet. For the best benefits, try to use whole-grain rice, pasta, and flour, because the energy from these foods is released more slowly in the body, making you feel fuller for longer.
- Eat more fruit and vegetables, aiming for at least five portions of different fruit and vegetables a day (excluding potatoes)—but don't fall into the trap of adding extra fat in the form of cream, butter, or oil. Not only can eating more fruit and vegetables help reduce your fat intake, they can increase the amount of fiber and vitamins you consume.

cutting down on unnecessary calories

Eating fewer sugary foods, such as cookies, cakes, and candy bars, will help reduce your sugar and fat intake. If you want something sweet, you should aim for fresh or dried fruit instead.

Reduce the amount of fat in your diet, so you consume fewer calories. Choose lean cuts of meat, such as Canadian bacon instead of typical fatty bacon, and chicken breasts instead of thighs. Trim all visible fat off meat before cooking and avoid frying foods—broil or roast instead. Fish is also naturally low in fat and can make a variety of tempting dishes.

Low-fat versions are available for most types of dairy products, including milk, cheese, yogurt, and even cream and butter. However, low-fat products are normally laden with sugar to make them taste better, so it's important to check labels carefully.

simple steps to reduce your calorie intake

Few of us have an iron will, so when you are trying to cut down, make it easier on yourself by following these steps:

- Serve small servings to start with. You may feel satisfied when you have finished, but if you are still hungry, you can always go back for more.
- Once you have served your meal, put away any leftover food before you eat. Don't put serving dishes with mounds of food on the table, because you will undoubtedly pick, even if you feel satisfied with what you have already eaten.
- Eat slowly and savor your food, which should help you to feel more full when you finish eating. If you rush a meal, you may still feel hungry afterward.
- Make an effort with your meals. Just because you are cutting down doesn't mean your meals have to be low on taste as well as calories. You will feel more satisfied with a meal you have really enjoyed and will be less tempted to look for comfort in a bag of potato chips or a bar of chocolate.
- Plan your meals in advance to make sure you have all the ingredients you need. Searching the cupboards when you are hungry is unlikely to result in a healthy, balanced meal.

- Keep healthy and interesting snacks on hand for those moments when you need something to pep you up. You don't need to succumb to a chocolate bar if there are other tempting treats available.

sugar

Experts believe it is possible for us as humans to become addicted to sugar, and with an increase in the rates of obesity, diabetes, and heart disease in the United States, it's time to look at how we can reduce our intake of a food that we really don't need in our daily diets. Sugar contains no nutrients other than calories, so it provides no protein, vitamins, minerals, or essential fats, just pure energy—which is great if you are intending to burn it off, but a lot of us don't, and then it becomes a problem.

how our bodies use sugar

Our bodies digest the sugars we eat using enzymes and acids, finally breaking it down to another type of sugar, called glucose. The stomach and intestines absorb the glucose and then release it into the bloodstream and, once there, it can be used immediately for energy or stored in the liver and muscle as glycogen for later use.

Insulin (which is made in the pancreas) helps to control the amount of glucose in the bloodstream. It tells the cells to let glucose in when there is too much of it in the bloodstream. As glucose moves from the bloodstream into the cells, blood sugar levels start to drop. The rise and fall of insulin and blood sugar goes on throughout the day and night, and it depends on how much, what, and when we eat.

Using glucose for energy and keeping it balanced with just the right amount of insulin is important for helping our bodies function perfectly. The body maintains a minimum level of glucose in the blood, about 70 mg/dl, and also regulates surges of glucose when you eat a meal to not exceed 140 mg/dl. To conserve fuel, the body stores excess glucose in the liver and muscles as glycogen. This can then be used when there is no glucose available.

simple and complex sugars

Simple sugars, such as pure sugar, honey, and syrups metabolize quickly and cause rapid spikes in blood sugar levels, whereas complex sugars, such as those found in

starchy vegetables, grains, and cereals, take longer to digest and, therefore, give a steadier blood sugar level throughout the day, along with sustained energy. Complex sugars also tend to provide more vitamins and minerals than simple sugars.

how much sugar should we consume?

It is currently recommended that no more than 10 percent of our diet should be from added sugar—the amount our body can store as glycogen without it turning to fat. This percentage doesn't include sugar that occurs naturally in foods with complex carbohydrates. Fruit, for example, contains fructose (fruit sugar), but whole fruit also contains fiber, which offsets the fructose and makes it healthier for our bodies.

Present surveys show that regardless of the age group, people are consuming 11.5–15.6 percent of their diets from added sugar—with soft drinks, candy, jelly, and alcohol being the biggest culprits.

Scientists are still investigating whether there are direct causal links between high sugar intake and weight gain, type 2 diabetes, heart disease, and other illnesses. What is known is that eating too many calories without burning them off through exercise can lead to obesity, and obesity is a risk factor for other diseases.

how to reduce the sugar in your diet

It's important to realize that sugar is in many foods you may not suspect it to be—store-bought soups, sauces, baked beans, cereals, flavored yogurts, and even your Chinese takeout—all contain unnecessary sugar that will add toward your daily total.

Cooking fresh ingredients from scratch enables you to be in control of any added

sugars, and once you start reducing them, you will find it becomes easier to go without. Most sugary snacks are eaten out of habit, because they are easily available, so instead be organized and prepared with foods that do not contain sugar. Here are a few tips:

- Cut out added sugar; use only honey and maple syrup in small amounts.
- Don't consume store-bought sauces or soups—they normally contain sugar, although you may not taste it.
- Avoid reduced-fat foods, because these products are normally laden with sugar to make them taste better.
- Use herbs and spices for giving extra flavor to your food.
- Choose fresh fruit snacks with small handfuls of nuts or seeds; eating protein with every meal and snack is not only more satiating, it also prevents spikes in blood sugar levels.
- Be aware that even so-called healthy breakfast cereals sometimes contain sugar—check the label be purchasing.

You can make your own sugar-free breakfast cereal by mixing rolled oats, nuts, and seeds together and soaking the mixture in milk in the refrigerator overnight.

- Cinnamon has been shown to help reduce sugar cravings, so use this warm spice to flavor your cooking and reduce sugar.
- Drink alcohol in moderation.
- Make a batch of healthy snacks, such as Fruit & Nut Bars (see page 38), so you have something to take to work each day instead of being tempted by store-bought cakes or other sweet treats.
- Drink herbal teas and water with slices of lemon or ginger instead of carbonated beverages or tea/coffee with sugar.

weight loss

Cutting down on your sugar intake should assist with weight loss, but it's still important to eat a healthy, balanced diet, one that includes great protein from meat, fish, eggs, beans and other legumes, nuts and seeds, and fresh fruit and vegetables. This book gives a variety of recipes for meals and snacks—and variety

in your diet is important to make sure you are consuming a wide range of nutrients that are all-important for optimum health.

Store-bought foods may contain more sugar to give them extra taste and texture, so again, cooking from scratch enables you to be in control of what you eat and makes it easier to be aware of how much sugar and calories you consume. Serving sizes are also important, and in this book a calorie intake is given for each recipe to help you to make great-tasting dishes from less than 200 to less than 500 calories per serving. If you include snacks in your daily intake, just be sure they are healthy choices.

When you are trying to lose weight, the key is to make conscious choices about eating whole, nutritious foods, with a diet that suits your lifestyle, and including exercise to balance what you eat.

less than 200 calories

pea, feta & spinach salad

Calories per serving **199**
Serves **4**
Preparation time **10 minutes,
 plus cooling**
Cooking time **2–3 minutes**

2 tablespoons **pumpkin
 seeds**
1 cup **fresh** or **frozen peas**
12 sprigs of **watercress** or
 1 cup other **peppery greens**
3 tablespoons **no-added-
 sugar mayonnaise**
1 teaspoon **no-added-sugar
 creamed horseradish**
6 oz **feta cheese**, cubed
2 cups **baby spinach leaves**
small handful of **mint leaves**
salt and **black pepper**

Heat a nonstick skillet over medium-low heat and dry-fry the pumpkin seeds for 2–3 minutes, stirring frequently, until slightly golden and toasted. Let cool.

Meanwhile, cook the peas in a saucepan of boiling water until tender. Drain and let cool.

Put the watercress, mayonnaise, and creamed horseradish into a food processor or blender and process until well combined. Season to taste, transfer to a bowl, and set aside.

Mix together the feta, peas, spinach, mint leaves, and pumpkin seeds in a bowl, then divide among 4 plates and serve with the watercress mayonnaise.

For pea, mint & feta soup, heat 1 tablespoon olive oil in a saucepan, add 1 chopped onion, and cook for 4–5 minutes, until softened, then add 1¾ cups frozen peas, 1 peeled and diced potato, and 2 cups vegetable broth and bring to a boil. Reduce the heat and simmer for 4–5 minutes, until the potato is tender. Add a small handful of mint leaves, then using a handheld blender, blend until smooth. Ladle into 4 bowls and serve sprinkled with ½ cup crumbled feta. **Calories per serving 163**

spicy seared squid & herb salad

Calories per serving **174**
Serves **4**
Preparation time **15 minutes,**
   plus marinating
Cooking time **10 minutes**

large pinch of **sea salt**
1 teaspoon **ground coriander**
1 teaspoon **ground cumin**
1 teaspoon **hot chili powder**
½ cup **lemon juice**
1 teaspoon **tomato paste**
1 **red chile,** seeded and
   finely sliced
1 teaspoon peeled and finely
   grated **fresh ginger root**
1 **garlic clove,** crushed
1½ lb **squid,** cut into
   bite-size pieces
1 small **red onion,** thinly sliced
large handful of **cilantro**
   leaves, chopped
small handful of **mint leaves,**
   chopped

Mix the salt, ground spices, chili powder, lemon juice, tomato paste, chile, ginger, and garlic in a large bowl and add the squid. Toss to coat evenly, cover, and let stand at room temperature for 15 minutes.

Heat a nonstick ridged grill pan over a high heat. Working in batches, lift the squid from the marinade and sear in the hot pan for 1–2 minutes, then remove from the pan and keep warm while you cook the remaining squid.

Add the red onion and herbs to the cooked squid, toss to mix well, and serve immediately.

For jumbo shrimp, mango & herb salad, replace the squid with 1½ lb peeled jumbo shrimp. Marinate in the spice mixture for 10 minutes, then cook in the smoking hot pan, in batches, for 2–3 minutes on each side, or until pink and cooked through. Transfer to a wide salad bowl and stir in a large handful each of cilantro and mint leaves and the diced flesh of 1 mango. Toss to mix well and serve. **Calories per serving 185**

lemon grass, shrimp & mint soup

Calories per serving **169**
Serves **4**
Preparation time **15 minutes**
Cooking time **10 minutes**

1 1/4 lb large **shrimp**, shells on
6 1/3 cups **water**
3 tablespoons **soy sauce**
3 **lemon grass stalks**, bruised
1 inch piece of **fresh ginger
    root**, peeled and sliced
1 **red chile,** seeded and sliced
4 **kaffir lime leaves**, shredded
3 1/2 oz **rice noodles**
2 tablespoons shredded **mint
lime** wedges, to serve
    (optional)

Peel the shrimp and set aside. Put the shells, heads, and tails into a saucepan and heat until the shells are well colored. Add the measured water and bring to a boil, then reduce the heat and simmer for 2 minutes. Strain through a strainer and return the broth to the pan, discarding the contents of the strainer.

Add the soy sauce, lemon grass, ginger, chile, and lime leaves to the broth and simmer for 5 minutes.

Meanwhile, cook the rice noodles according to the package directions.

Add the shrimp to the broth and cook for 2–3 minutes, until they turn pink and are cooked through.

Divide the rice noodles among 4 bowls. Stir the mint into the soup, then pour it over the noodles. Serve with lime wedges for squeezing over the soup, if desired.

For asparagus, lemon grass & shrimp stir-fry, mix together 1 tablespoon peeled and grated fresh ginger root, 1 bruised and finely chopped lemon grass stalk, 4 sliced lime leaves, and 3 tablespoons no-added-sugar Thai fish sauce. Heat a wok and add 1 tablespoon peanut oil. Cook 10 peeled jumbo shrimp for 2–3 minutes, until they turn pink, then remove from the pan. Add 1 sliced onion, 2 sliced red chiles, 3 chopped scallions, and 3 chopped garlic cloves to the pan and stir-fry for 4 minutes. Return the shrimp to the pan with 8 oz trimmed and halved asparagus stems and cook for 1 minute. Pour in the spiced sauce and cook for another 1 minute, then serve. **Calories per serving 107**

avocado & sour cream soup

Calories per serving **170**
Serves **6**
Preparation time **15 minutes**
Cooking time **5 minutes**

1 tablespoon **sunflower oil**
4 **scallions**, sliced, plus
  2 extra to garnish
2 large ripe **avocados**,
  halved and pitted
¼ cup **sour cream**
2½ cups **vegetable** or
  chicken broth
juice of 2 **limes**
few drops of **Tabasco sauce**
salt and **black pepper**
ice cubes, to serve

Heat the oil in a skillet, add the scallions, and sauté for 5 minutes, until softened. Set aside.

Cut extremely thin strips from the 2 extra scallions to create curls. Soak in cold water for 10 minutes, then drain.

Scoop out the avocado flesh from the shells and add to a blender or food processor with the fried scallions, the sour cream, and about one-third of the broth. Blend to a smooth puree, then gradually mix in the remaining broth and lime juice. Season to taste with salt, black pepper, and a few drops of Tabasco sauce.

Serve the soup immediately, while the avocado is still bright green, in 6 cups or glasses containing some ice. Sprinkle the scallion curls over the soup.

For homemade salt & pepper grissini, to serve as an accompaniment, put 1¾ cups plus 1 tablespoon white bread flour into a bowl and mix with ¼ teaspoon salt, 1 teaspoon maple syrup, and 1 teaspoon active dry yeast. Add 4 teaspoons olive oil and gradually mix in up to ⅔ cup warm water to form a smooth dough. Knead for 5 minutes on a lightly floured surface, then cut the dough into 18 pieces and roll each into a thin rope. Place on a greased baking sheet, cover with oiled plastic wrap, and let rest in a warm place to rise for 30 minutes. Remove the plastic wrap, brush the bread with beaten egg, then sprinkle with a little coarse sea salt and a generous sprinkling of coarsely crushed black peppercorns. Bake in a preheated oven, at 400°F, for 6–8 minutes, until golden. Serve warm or cold with the soup. **Calories per grissini 57**

scallops with minty pea puree

Calories per serving **152**
Serves **4**
Preparation time **5 minutes**
Cooking time **10 minutes**

2 tablespoons **olive oil**
4 **shallots**, finely diced
2 cups **frozen peas**
½ cup **fish broth**
small handful of **mint leaves**
1 tablespoon **crème fraîche**
grated zest and juice of
  1 **lemon**
12 cleaned **scallops**
salt and **black pepper**

Heat 1 tablespoon of the oil in a small saucepan, add the shallots, and sauté for 4–5 minutes, until softened. Stir in the peas and broth and cook until the peas are heated through. Transfer to a food processor or blender, add the mint leaves, crème fraîche, lemon zest, and salt and black pepper, and blend until smooth.

Meanwhile, heat the remaining oil in a skillet or ridged grill pan, add the scallops, and cook for 2 minutes on each side, until cooked through, squeezing with lemon juice after turning them over.

Divide the pea puree among 4 plates, top with the scallops, and drizzle with the cooking juices.

For pan-fried scallops with lime & cilantro, heat 1 tablespoon olive oil in a skillet, add 12 cleaned scallops, and cook for 2 minutes. Flip over the scallops, sprinkle with 2 large chopped garlic cloves and 1 seeded and chopped red chile, and cook for 1 minute, until just cooked through. Squeeze the juice of 1 lime over the top, then stir in a handful of chopped cilantro and season with salt and black pepper. Serve immediately. **Calories per serving 69**

poached chicken & vegetables

Calories per serving **195**
Serves **4**
Preparation time **10 minutes**
Cooking time **25 minutes**

2 **fennel bulbs**, thinly sliced
4 **boneless, skinless chicken
   breasts** (about 5 oz each),
   sliced diagonally into
   3 pieces
grated zest and juice of
   1 lemon
2½ cups **chicken broth**
1 **zucchini**, sliced
2 tablespoons chopped
   parsley

Put the fennel, chicken, lemon zest and juice, and broth into a wok or large saucepan and bring to a boil, then reduce the heat and simmer, uncovered, for 15 minutes.

Add the zucchini and half the parsley and cook for another 5 minutes, until the zucchini is tender and the chicken is cooked through.

Serve sprinkled with the remaining parsley.

For lemon, zucchini & chicken pasta, cook 11½ oz gluten-free whole-grain pasta in a saucepan of boiling water according to the package directions. Meanwhile, heat 1 tablespoon butter in a skillet, add 3 shredded zucchini, and sauté for 5 minutes, until softened. Add 1½ cups shredded, cooked chicken and cook for 2–3 minutes, until heated through. Drain the pasta, then stir into the chicken mixture with 2 tablespoons olive oil, 4 thinly sliced scallions, the juice and grated zest of 1 lemon, and black pepper. **Calories per serving 476**

ranch-style eggs

Calories per serving **188**
Serves **4**
Preparation time **10 minutes**
Cooking time **15 minutes**

2 tablespoons **olive oil**
1 **onion**, finely sliced
1 **red chile**, seeded and
   finely chopped
1 **garlic clove**, crushed
1 teaspoon **ground cumin**
1 teaspoon **dried oregano**
1 ½ cups canned **cherry
   tomatoes**
1 (7 oz) jar **roasted red** and
   yellow bell peppers in
   oil, drained and coarsely
   chopped
4 **eggs**
salt and **black pepper**
¼ cup finely chopped **cilantro**,
   to garnish

Heat the oil in a large skillet, add the onion, chile, garlic, cumin, and oregano, and sauté gently for about 5 minutes, until softened.

Add the tomatoes and roasted peppers and cook for another 5 minutes. If the sauce looks dry, add a splash of water.

Season well and make 4 hollows in the mixture, then break an egg into each and cover the pan. Cook for 5 minutes, or until the eggs are just set.

Serve immediately, garnished with the chopped cilantro and sprinkled with extra black pepper.

For Mexican-style scrambled eggs, heat

1 tablespoon each olive oil and butter in a large skillet. Whisk together 8 eggs, 1 crushed garlic clove, 1 finely chopped red chile, 1 teaspoon dried oregano, and 1 teaspoon ground cumin in a bowl. Season, pour into the skillet, and cook over medium-low heat, stirring frequently, until the eggs are scrambled and cooked to your preference. Serve sprinkled with chopped cilantro.
Calories per serving 230

eggplant curry

Calories per serving **108**
Serves **4**
Preparation time **10 minutes**
Cooking time **35–40 minutes**

2 **eggplants** (about 1¾ lb)
1 tablespoon **olive oil**
1 **onion**, sliced
1 **green chile,** seeded
  and sliced
2 **garlic cloves,** crushed
1 inch piece of **fresh ginger
  root,** peeled and shredded
1²⁄₃ cups canned **diced
  tomatoes**
1 tablespoon **tomato paste**
1 teaspoon **ground cumin**
1 teaspoon **ground coriander**
small bunch of **cilantro,**
  chopped
salt and **black pepper**
¼ cup **low-fat plain yogurt,**
  to serve

Prick the eggplants all over with a fork and bake in a preheated oven, at 425°F, for 20 minutes, until the skin is blackened. When cool enough to handle, peel off the skin and coarsely chop the flesh.

Heat the oil in a skillet, add the onion, and sauté for 3–4 minutes, until starting to soften. Stir in the chile, garlic, and ginger and cook for another 2–3 minutes.

Add the eggplant, diced tomatoes, tomato paste, and dried spices and cook for another 10–12 minutes. Season to taste, then stir in the chopped cilantro.

Serve with dollops of plain yogurt.

For baba ganoush, prick 2 large eggplants all over with a fork. Broil or bake as above for 15–20 minutes, until the skins are blackened and the flesh feels soft. Put 2 peeled garlic cloves, the juice of 1 lemon, 2 tablespoons tahini, 2 tablespoons olive oil, and salt and black pepper into a food processor or blender and blend together. When cool enough to handle, cut the eggplants in half and scoop out the flesh. Mix with the smooth paste and serve with a sprinkling of chopped parsley. **Calories per serving 137**

vegetable stroganoff

Calories per serving **159**
Serves **4**
Preparation time **15 minutes**
Cooking time **20 minutes**

1 tablespoon **olive oil**
1 **onion**, diced
2 **garlic cloves**, finely chopped
1 ¼ cups peeled, seeded, and
   diced **butternut squash**
1 **carrot**, peeled and diced
⅔ cup peeled and diced
   celeriac
3½ oz **shiitake mushrooms**,
   sliced
½ teaspoon **paprika**
1 cup **vegetable broth**
1½ cups rinsed, drained
   canned **kidney beans**
2 tablespoons **plain yogurt**
2 tablespoons chopped
   parsley
salt and **black pepper**

Heat the oil in a saucepan, add the onion and garlic, and sauté for 2 minutes, until starting to soften. Add the butternut, carrot, celeriac, mushrooms, and paprika and cook for another 2–3 minutes.

Pour in the broth, cover, and simmer for 10 minutes, then add the beans and cook for another 5 minutes, until all the vegetables are tender.

Stir in the yogurt and parsley and season to taste.

For roasted vegetable salad, toss together the onion, garlic, butternut squash, and celeriac in a large bowl, then add 2 peeled and diced carrots and 1 thickly sliced zucchini. Toss together with 2 tablespoons olive oil and 1 teaspoon smoked paprika. Divide between 2 roasting pans and roast in a preheated oven, at 400°F, for 30–35 minutes, until tender. Toss the roasted vegetables with 3½ cups baby spinach leaves and serve with a squeeze of lemon juice and grinding of black pepper. **Calories per serving 80**

fruit & nut bars

Calories per slice **99**
Makes **16**
Preparation time **10 minutes**
Cooking time **20 minutes**

butter, for greasing
1 large **carrot**, peeled and
   chopped
1 **sweet, crisp apple**,
   quartered and cored
½ teaspoon **ground
   cinnamon**
½ teaspoon **ground nutmeg**
1 cup **cooked brown rice**
2 **eggs**
⅓ cup **water**
¾ cup **rice flour**
⅓ cup **raisins**
½ cup chopped **hazelnuts**
1 tablespoon **sesame seeds**

Grease a 12 x 8 inch baking pan and line with nonstick parchment paper.

Put the carrot, apple, spices, rice, eggs, and measured water into a food processor or blender and blend until smooth. Add the rice flour and blend again, then add the raisins and nuts and process for 10 seconds, until just chopped.

Transfer the dough to the prepared pan, sprinkle with the sesame seeds, and mark into 16 bars. Bake in a preheated oven, at 400°F, for 20 minutes, until lightly golden. Let cool in the pan, then remove the lining paper and break into bars. Store in an airtight container and eat within 3–4 days.

For fruit & nut bircher muesli, mix 2⅓ cups rolled oats with 2 tablespoons raisins, 2 tablespoons chopped pitted dates, 1 tablespoon pumpkin seeds, 1 tablespoon toasted walnut halves, 1 teaspoon ground cinnamon, 1 tablespoon chopped hazelnuts, and 1 tablespoon dry unsweetened coconut in a bowl. Grate 1 sweet, crisp apple into the mixture, stir in 1¼ cups low-fat milk, and let soak in the refrigerator overnight. Divide the muesli among 4 bowls, top each with a handful of fresh berries, and serve with extra milk, if desired. **Calories per serving 173 (not including extra milk)**

poppy seed & lemon cupcakes

Calories per cake **170**
Makes **12**
Preparation time **20 minutes,
    plus cooling**
Cooking time about **1 hour**

2 **unwaxed lemons**
1 cup **ground hazelnuts**
½ cup **spelt flour**
1 teaspoon **baking powder**
2 tablespoons **poppy seeds**
3 **eggs**
5 tablespoons **agave nectar**,
    plus extra for drizzling
3½ tablespoons **salted butter**,
    melted
⅓ cup **golden raisins**

Line a 12-cup muffin pan with paper cupcake liners. Cut one lemon into 12 thin slices. Put with the whole lemon into a small saucepan and cover with boiling water. Simmer gently for 20–30 minutes, until the slices are tender. Drain the slices and reserve. Cook the whole lemon for another 15 minutes, until soft and squashy. Drain and let cool.

Halve the whole lemon and discard the seeds. Coarsely chop, put into a food processor or blender, and blend to a puree.

Mix the ground hazelnuts in a bowl with the flour, baking powder, and poppy seeds. Mix the eggs with the lemon puree, agave nectar, and melted butter and add to the dry ingredients with the golden raisins. Stir until evenly combined.

Divide the cake batter among the paper liners and place a reserved lemon slice on top. Drizzle each lemon slice with a little extra agave nectar.

Bake in a preheated oven, at 350°F, for 20 minutes, or until risen and lightly browned. Transfer to a wire rack to cool.

For Brazil nut & orange cupcakes, cook 1 small orange as above. Drain, put into a food processor or blender with the eggs, melted butter, agave nectar, and golden raisins, and blend to a puree. Chop and then grind 20 shelled Brazil nuts. Mix with the flour and baking powder as above, adding ½ teaspoon ground allspice (omit the poppy seeds). Combine with the orange puree and bake as above, with a whole Brazil nut on top of each cake. **Calories per cake 180**

banana & raspberry ice cream

Calories per serving **92**
  (including maple syrup)
Serves **4**
Preparation time **10 minutes,**
  plus freezing

2 **bananas**, cut into ¼ inch
  slices
¾ cup **raspberries**
2 tablespoons **coconut**
  cream (removed from the
  top of a can of coconut milk,
  not sweetened cream of
  coconut)
1 tablespoon **maple syrup**
  (optional)

Place the banana slices in a single layer on a tray, then put into the freezer with the raspberries and freeze for at least 2 hours.

Put a few of the frozen banana pieces into a food processor and process, then with the motor still running, gradually add more banana pieces, a few raspberries, a drizzle of coconut cream, and maple syrup, if using, through the feeder tube. Continue to add the ingredients until they are all used and the ice cream is thick and creamy.

Serve immediately or transfer to a freezer-proof container and put into the freezer for up to 1 hour before serving. (If left in the freezer too long, the ice cream will set hard and will need to be left at room temperature for about 20 minutes before serving.)

For banana & mango ice cream, slice 3 bananas and freeze in a single layer as above. Peel, pit, and dice 1 large mango, then freeze as above. Pour ½ cup plus 1 tablespoon almond milk into a food processor and turn on to full power. Gradually add the banana and mango pieces as above and blend until the ice cream is smooth and creamy. **Calories per serving 119**

berry & mint compote

Calories per serving **97**
Serves **4**
Preparation time **5 minutes,
   plus cooling**
Cooking time **12–15 minutes**

1 (14½ oz) package **mixed
   fruit**, such as strawberries,
   blackberries, raspberries,
   and halved and pitted plums
1 **cinnamon stick**
grated zest and juice of
   1 orange
8 **mint leaves**, shredded
1 ⅓ cups **plain yogurt**,
   to serve (optional)

Put the fruit, cinnamon stick, and orange zest and juice into a small saucepan and simmer gently for 12–15 minutes.

Remove the cinnamon stick and let the compote cool for 3–4 minutes, then stir in the mint. Spoon into 4 bowls, divide the plain yogurt among them, if desired, and serve.

For berry & mint smoothies, put 1⅔ cups plain yogurt, 1⅔ cups soy milk, 5–6 ice cubes, 2¼ cups mixed raspberries, blueberries, and hulled strawberries, and 5–6 mint leaves in a food processor or blender and blend until smooth. Pour into 4 glasses and serve topped with mint sprigs. **Calories per serving 119**

melon with mint & ginger syrup

Calories per serving **108**

Serves **4**

Preparation time **5 minutes, plus standing**

Cooking time **5 minutes**

1 tablespoon **sesame seeds**

1/2 **honeydew melon**, peeled, seeded, and cut into large chunks

1/2 **cantaloupe**, peeled, seeded, and cut into large chunks

3 tablespoons **maple syrup**

1 tablespoon **water**

2 tablespoons **shredded mint**

1 tablespoon peeled and shredded **fresh ginger root**

Heat a nonstick skillet over medium-low heat and dry-fry the sesame seeds for 2 minutes, stirring frequently, until golden brown and toasted. Set aside.

Place the melon chunks on a large serving plate.

Pour the maple syrup into a saucepan with the measured water and bring to a boil, then add the mint and ginger and turn off the heat. Let stand for 5 minutes, then pour the syrup over the melon.

Sprinkle with the toasted sesame seeds and serve.

For melon & ginger smoothies, put the flesh of 1 cantaloupe into a blender with 1/2 teaspoon ground ginger, a pinch of nutmeg, 2 tablespoons Greek yogurt, and 3¾ cups low-fat milk. Blend until smooth, then pour into 4 glasses and serve. **Calories per serving 157**

banana rice pudding

Calories per serving **162**
Serves **4**
Preparation time **5 minutes**
Cooking time about **2 hours**

butter, for greasing
½ cup small, broken
  dried banana pieces
¼ cup **short-grain rice**
3 cups **milk**
large pinch of freshly grated
  nutmeg

Grease a 1 quart ovenproof dish lightly with butter and put the banana pieces and rice into the dish.

Heat the milk in a small saucepan until it reaches boiling point, then pour it over the bananas and rice and stir to mix. Sprinkle with the grated nutmeg.

Bake in a preheated oven, at 300°F, for 1¾–2 hours, until the rice is tender and most of the milk has been absorbed, stirring once halfway through cooking.

For quick banana mousse, mash 4 ripe bananas with 2 tablespoons maple syrup or honey in a bowl. Stir in 2 cups Greek yogurt, then spoon evenly into 4 bowls or glasses and top with 1 tablespoon broken dried banana pieces. **Calories per serving 251**

mixed fruit salad

Calories per serving **125**
Serves **6**
Preparation time **15 minutes**

¼ small **watermelon**, peeled
  and seeded
½ **galia** or **honeydew melon**,
  peeled and seeded
1 **mango**, peeled and pitted
2 **green crisp, sweet apples**,
  quartered and cored
2 **bananas**
3 **kiwifruit**, peeled
7 oz **strawberries** (about
  1 ¼ cups prepared)
1 cup **blueberries**

Cut the melon flesh into 1 inch chunks and put into a large bowl.

Dice the mango and apples, then slice the bananas. Add to the bowl with the melon.

Cut the kiwifruit flesh into slices, then hull and halve the strawberries. Add the kiwifruit, strawberries, and blueberries to the bowl and mix the fruit together gently.

For passion fruit cream, to serve as an accompaniment, whisk together ¼ cup mascarpone cheese and 1 cup heavy cream in a bowl until soft peaks form. Gently fold in the pulp of 2 passion fruit. **Calories per serving 197**

lemon & blueberry pancakes

Calories per pancake **107**
Makes **12**
Preparation time **10 minutes**
Cooking time **10–20 minutes**

2 cups **whole-wheat flour**
2 teaspoons **baking powder**
grated zest of **1 lemon**
2 **eggs**, beaten
1¼ cups **low-fat milk**
2 cups **blueberries**

To serve
lemon juice
2 tablespoons **maple syrup**

Put the flour, baking powder, and lemon zest into a bowl and make a well in the center. Pour the eggs into the well, then whisk together, gradually adding the milk to form a smooth batter. Stir in half the blueberries.

Heat a nonstick skillet over medium heat, add 3–4 tablespoons of the batter to form individual pancakes, and cook for 1–2 minutes, until golden underneath, then flip over and cook for another 1–2 minutes. Remove from the pan and keep warm. Repeat with the remaining batter to make 12 pancakes.

Serve sprinkled with the remaining blueberries, a squeeze of lemon juice, and drizzle of maple syrup.

For lemon & blueberry cups, lightly crush 2 cups blueberries in a bowl until some of them burst. Stir in 2 cups Greek yogurt and the grated zest of 1 lemon. Divide among 4 small glasses or bowls and sprinkle with 1 tablespoon toasted slivered almonds to serve. **Calories per serving 194**

chargrilled fruit with spicy salt

Calories per serving **72**
Serves **6**
Preparation time **15 minutes**
Cooking time **6 minutes**

1 large **mango**, peeled and
    pitted
½ **pineapple**, skin removed
    and cored
2 **bananas**
½ teaspoon **dried red**
    pepper flakes
1 tablespoon **sea salt** or
    vanilla sea salt

Cut the mango into ¾ inch pieces and the pineapple into small wedges. Cut the bananas into thick slices.

Thread the fruit onto 6 metal or presoaked wooden skewers, alternating the fruits.

Mix together the dried red pepper flakes and salt and set aside.

Heat a ridged grill pan over medium heat, add the skewers, and cook for 3 minutes on each side, until golden and caramelized. Remove the skewers from the pan, sprinkle with the spicy salt mix, and serve.

For vanilla sea salt, to accompany the skewers, scrape the seeds of 1 vanilla bean into a small bowl with ¼ cup sea salt. Stir to combine well and let infuse for at least 2 hours. **Calories per serving negligible**

papaya with tumbling berries

Calories per serving **92**
   (not including honey)
Serves **4**
Preparation time **8 minutes**

2 large **papayas**
1 cup **blueberries**
1 cup **raspberries**
1²/₃ cups sliced, hulled
   strawberries
¾ cup pitted **cherries**
honey, to taste (optional)
lime wedges, to serve

Cut the papayas in half, then scoop out the seeds and discard. Place each half on a serving plate.

Mix together the blueberries, raspberries, strawberries, and cherries in a bowl and then pile into the papaya halves. Drizzle with a little honey, if desired, and serve with lime wedges.

For papaya & berry smoothies, peel and halve the papayas, remove the seeds, and cut into chunks. Put into a food processor or blender with the remaining fruits and 10 ice cubes. Add 2 cups pure apple or guava juice and blend until smooth. Pour into 4 glasses and serve immediately. **Calories per serving 144**

pineapple & grapefruit with mint

Calories per serving **161**
Serves **4**
Preparation time **10 minutes,**
  plus cooling
Cooking time **5 minutes**

2 tablespoons **honey**
juice of ½ **lime**
1 tablespoon **water**
2 **pink grapefruits**
1 small **pineapple**
small bunch of **mint**, leaves
  only, shredded
¼ cup **plain yogurt**, to serve

Put the honey, lime juice, and measured water into a small saucepan and slowly bring to a simmer, then stir, turn off the heat, and let cool.

Remove the grapefruit sections over a bowl to catch the juices. Remove the skin from the pineapple, cut into quarters, and remove the core. Cut into thin slices, adding any juice to the grapefruit juices. Arrange the fruit on a serving platter.

Stir the reserved fruit juices and the mint into the honey mixture, then pour it over the fruit. Serve with the plain yogurt.

For glazed spiced pineapple, mix together the juice and grated zest of 1 lime, 2 tablespoons honey, and a couple of pinches of ground cinnamon in a bowl. Peel and core 1 pineapple as above, then cut into 8 wedges. Heat 4 teaspoons butter in a skillet and cook the pineapple wedges for 3–4 minutes, turning frequently, until caramelized. Pour in the spiced lime sauce and let simmer for a few seconds, turning the pineapple in the sauce. Divide among 4 plates and serve each with 1 tablespoon crème fraîche or Greek yogurt. **Calories per serving 385**

spicy melon foam

Calories per serving **72**
Serves **6**
Preparation time **15 minutes**

2 **Galia** or **honeydew melons**
juice of **1 lime**
½–1 large mild **red chile,**
    seeded and quartered
small bunch of **cilantro**, plus
    extra sprigs to decorate
1¼ cups **apple cider** or
    apple juice
ice cubes, to serve
lime wedges, to decorate
    (optional)

Cut the melons in half, scoop out and discard the seeds, then scoop the flesh away from the skin and put it into a blender or food processor with the lime juice, chile, and cilantro, torn into pieces. Add half the apple cider and blend until smooth. Gradually mix in the remaining juice until frothy.

Pour the melon foam into 6 cups or glasses filled halfway with ice and serve immediately, decorated with a sprig of cilantro and lime wedges, if desired, before the foamy texture loses its bubbles.

balsamic & pepper strawberries

Calories per serving **41**
Serves **4**
Preparation time **5 minutes**

1 lb **strawberries**, hulled and
  halved
2 tablespoons **balsamic
  vinegar**
1 teaspoon freshly ground
  black pepper

Place the strawberries in a bowl and pour the vinegar
over the fruit.

Stir well to incorporate the flavors, then add the black
pepper to taste. Serve immediately.

apple & pear tart

Calories per serving **152**
Serves **8**
Preparation time **15 minutes**
Cooking time **10–15 minutes**

¾ cup plus 1 tablespoon
   rice flour
1½ cups **ground almonds
   (almond meal)**
1 tablespoon **tahini**
1½ teaspoons **sunflower oil**
½ cup **cold water**
4 **sweet, crisp apples**, peeled,
   cored, and chopped
2 **pitted dates**
1½ teaspoons **ground
   cinnamon**
2 **pears**, peeled, cored,
   and thinly sliced
juice of **1 lemon**

Put the rice flour, ground almonds, tahini, and oil into a food processor and process until the mixture resembles bread crumbs. With the motor still running, slowly add the measured water though the feeder tube until the mixture comes together like pie dough.

Line an 8 inch tart pan with the dough, using your fingers to push it to the edges. Bake in a preheated oven, at 350°F, for 10–15 minutes, until golden.

Meanwhile, put the apples, dates, and 1 teaspoon of the cinnamon into a small saucepan with 2 tablespoons water and cook over gentle heat until the apples are soft. Transfer to a food processor or blender and blend to a puree, then spread over the bottom of the pastry shell.

Toss the pears in the lemon juice, then arrange them in a spiral over the apple mixture. Sprinkle with the remaining cinnamon to serve.

For apple & pear whip, peel, core, and chop 3 sweet, crisp apples and 2 pears. Put into a saucepan with 6 pitted dates, 1 teaspoon ground cinnamon, the grated zest and juice of 1 orange, and ⅔ cup water. Cook over a gentle heat until the apples and pears are soft. Blend as above until smooth and let cool. Fold into 2 cups low-fat plain yogurt and spoon into 4 glasses or bowls. Chill for 20 minutes before serving. **Calories per serving 213**

less than
300 calories

crab & grapefruit salad

Calories per serving **253**
Serves **4**
Preparation time **15 minutes**
Cooking time **2 minutes**

2 tablespoons **sesame seeds**
2 **pink grapefruits**
3 tablespoons **extra virgin olive oil**
1 teaspoon **honey**
1 teaspoon **Dijon mustard**
11½ oz **white crabmeat**
½ bunch of **watercress** or 2 cups other **peppery greens**
1½ cups **snow peas**
small handful of **cilantro leaves**
salt and **black pepper**

Heat a nonstick skillet over medium-low heat and dry-fry the sesame seeds for 2 minutes, stirring frequently, until golden brown and toasted. Set aside.

Remove the grapefruit sections over a bowl to catch the juice.

Whisk together 2 tablespoons of the grapefruit juice with the olive oil, honey, and mustard in a small bowl. Season with salt and black pepper.

Mix 1 tablespoon of the dressing with the crabmeat.

Divide the watercress, snow peas, grapefruit sections, and cilantro leaves among 4 plates and top with the crabmeat.

Sprinkle with the toasted sesame seeds and the remaining dressing and serve.

For spiced potted crab, mix together 10 oz crabmeat, 7 tablespoons melted butter, ½ seeded and finely chopped red chile, the juice of 1 lemon, ½ teaspoon grated nutmeg, and a pinch of salt in a bowl, then pack into a 12 oz jar. Melt 6 tablespoons butter until it is foaming. Remove from the heat and skim off the scum with a teaspoon. Pour the clear butter over the crab, top with a bay leaf, and let set in the refrigerator for 1 hour before serving with gluten-free crispbreads, if desired. **Calories per serving 384 (not including crispbreads)**

squash, kale & mixed bean soup

Calories per serving **243**
  (not including garlic bread)
Serves **6**
Preparation time **15 minutes**
Cooking time **40 minutes**

1 tablespoon **olive oil**
1 **onion**, finely chopped
2 **garlic cloves**, finely chopped
1 teaspoon **smoked paprika**
½ **butternut squash**, peeled,
  seeded, and diced
2 small **carrots**, peeled and
  diced
4 **tomatoes**, skinned, if
  preferred, and coarsely
  chopped
2 cups rinsed, drained canned
  mixed beans, such as pinto
  beans, kidney beans, and
  chickpeas
3¾ cups **vegetable** or
  chicken broth
⅔ cup **crème fraîche** or
  Greek yogurt
1½ cups **kale** (torn into
  bite-size pieces)
salt and **black pepper**

Heat the oil in a saucepan, add the onion, and sauté
gently for 5 minutes. Stir in the garlic and smoked
paprika and cook briefly, then add the squash, carrots,
tomatoes, and mixed beans.

Pour in the broth, season with salt and black pepper,
and bring to a boil, stirring. Cover and simmer for
25 minutes, until the vegetables are tender.

Stir the crème fraîche into the soup, then add the kale,
pressing it just beneath the surface of the broth. Cover
and cook for 5 minutes, until the kale has just wilted.
Ladle into 6 bowls and serve with warm garlic bread,
if desired.

For cheesy squash, red pepper & mixed bean soup,
sauté the onion in oil as above, add the garlic, smoked
paprika, squash, tomatoes, and beans, adding a cored,
seeded, and diced red pepper instead of the carrot. Pour
in the broth, then add 65 g (2½ oz) Parmesan rinds and
season. Cover and simmer for 25 minutes. Stir in the
crème fraîche but omit the kale. Discard the Parmesan
rinds, ladle the soup into 6 bowls, and top each with
3 tablespoons freshly grated Parmesan. **Calories per
serving 301**

potato & avocado salad

Calories per serving **281**
Serves **4**
Preparation time **10 minutes**
Cooking time **12–15 minutes**

1¼ lb small **new potatoes**
1 **avocado**
½ cup **garden cress** or
   other **microgreens**
grated zest of ½ **lemon**
3 cups **arugula leaves**
salt and **black pepper**

Dressing
1 tablespoon **no-added-sugar**
   whole-grain mustard
juice of ½ **lemon**
2 tablespoons **no-added-**
   sugar mayonnaise

Cook the potatoes in a saucepan of salted boiling water for 12–15 minutes, or until just tender. Drain well and place in a large salad bowl.

Halve the avocado, remove the pit, and peel. Cut the flesh into pieces. Whisk together the dressing ingredients in a small bowl, then add to the warm potatoes. Mix in the avocado pieces, cress, lemon zest, and arugula. Season well.

Divide the salad among 4 bowls or plates and serve.

For potato & sun-dried tomato salad, cook the potatoes as above, drain well, and place in a large salad bowl. While they are still warm, stir in 6 sliced, drained sun-dried tomatoes in oil, 12 sliced pitted olives, 2 tablespoons pesto, and 3 tablespoons light crème fraîche or Greek yogurt. Season with plenty of black pepper. **Calories per serving 252**

fennel vichyssoise

Calories per serving **209**
Serves **6**
Preparation time **20 minutes,
    plus chilling**
Cooking time **30 minutes**

2 tablespoons **butter**
1 **fennel bulb** (about 7–8 oz),
    green feathery tops trimmed
    and reserved, bulb coarsely
    chopped
4 **scallions**, thickly sliced
1 **Yukon gold** or **white round
    potato**, diced
2 cups **chicken broth**
1 cup **milk**
²/₃ cup **heavy cream**
salt and **black pepper**
ice cubes, to serve

Heat the butter in a saucepan, add the chopped fennel, scallions, and potato, toss in the butter, then cover and sauté gently for 10 minutes, stirring occasionally, until softened but not browned.

Pour in the broth, season, and bring to a boil. Cover and simmer for 15 minutes, until the vegetables are just tender and still tinged green.

Let the soup cool slightly, then puree, in batches, in a blender or food processor until smooth. Pour the puree through a fine strainer back into the saucepan, then press the coarser pieces of fennel through the strainer using the back of a ladle. Mix in the milk and cream, then taste and adjust the seasoning, if needed. Chill well.

Ladle the soup into 6 small bowls or cups filled halfway with ice and garnish with the reserved green feathery tops, snipped into small pieces.

For classic vichyssoise, omit the fennel and scallions and add 4 trimmed, cleaned, and sliced leeks. Stir half the cream into the soup and swirl the rest through the bowls before serving. Garnish with a sprinkling of a few snipped chives. **Calories per serving 215**

spinach & feta quiches

Calories per serving **274**
Serves **4**
Preparation time **15 minutes**
Cooking time **12–15 minutes**

1 (12 oz) package **fresh
  spinach**
6 **extra-large eggs**
½ cup **milk**
2 tablespoons grated
  Parmesan cheese
2 tablespoons chopped
  chives
3½ oz **feta cheese**, cubed
  or crumbled
8 **cherry tomatoes**, halved
salt and **black pepper**
crisp green salad, to serve

Put the spinach into a strainer and pour over boiling water to wilt. Squeeze out any excess liquid. Line 8 cups of a muffin pan with (6 inch squares of wax paper.

Beat together the eggs, milk, Parmesan, chives, and feta cheese in a small bowl and season with salt and black pepper.

Divide the spinach among the muffin liners, then pour in the egg mixture. Top each one with 2 tomato halves.

Bake in a preheated oven, at 350°F, for 12–15 minutes, until just set. Serve with a crisp green salad.

For spinach & feta frittata, whisk 7 extra-large eggs in a bowl and season with salt and black pepper. Heat 1 tablespoon olive oil in a skillet, add 4 sliced scallions, and cook for 2–3 minutes. Add 5 cups fresh spinach and toss in the hot oil to wilt. Add to the beaten eggs and mix well. Crumble in 7 oz feta cheese. Heat 1 tablespoon olive oil in the skillet, pour in the egg mixture, and cook over medium heat until nearly set, then place under a preheated hot broiler until cooked and golden on top. Serve cut into 4 wedges. **Calories per serving 345**

spicy falafel with mint raita

Calories per serving **212**
Serves **4**
Preparation time **15 minutes,
    plus chilling**
Cooking time **20 minutes**

2 tablespoons **peanut oil**
1 small **onion**, finely diced
2 **garlic cloves**, crushed
1²/₃ cups rinsed, drained
    canned **chickpeas**
    (garbanzo beans)
1 teaspoon **ground cumin**
½ teaspoon **ground coriander**
small handful of **cilantro**,
    chopped
small handful of **parsley**,
    chopped
salt and **black pepper**

Raita
1¼ cups **plain yogurt**
½ **cucumber**, grated
small handful of **mint**, chopped

Heat 1 tablespoon of the oil in a skillet, add the onion and garlic, and sauté for 4–5 minutes, until softened.

Transfer the onion and garlic to a food processor or blender, add the chickpeas, spices, and salt and black pepper, then process to a coarse mixture. Add the herbs and pulse until combined. Chill for 30 minutes.

Meanwhile, make the raita. Mix together the yogurt, cucumber, and mint in a bowl. Cover and chill.

Roll the chickpea mixture into about 32 balls, then flatten to make small patties. Heat the remaining oil in a skillet, add the patties, in batches if necessary, and cook for 3 minutes on each side, until golden and firm. Serve with the raita.

For chickpea & mint soup, heat 1 tablespoon olive oil in a skillet, add 1 chopped onion, 2 chopped celery sticks, and 2 chopped garlic cloves, and cook for 4–5 minutes, until softened. Add 1²/₃ cups rinsed, drained canned chickpeas (garbanzo beans), 1 chopped bunch of mint, ½ teaspoon ground cumin, 1 tablespoon tahini, and 3½ cups vegetable broth. Bring to a boil, then reduce the heat and simmer for 30 minutes. Season, then mash lightly with a vegetable masher. Ladle into 4 bowls and serve each topped with 3 tablespoons low-fat plain yogurt. **Calories per serving 192**

squash, carrot & mango tagine

Calories per serving **232**
 (not including couscous)
Serves **4**
Preparation time **15 minutes**
Cooking time **35–40 minutes**

2 tablespoons **olive oil**
1 large **onion**, cut into large
   chunks
3 **garlic cloves**, finely chopped
1 **butternut squash** (about
   1¾ lb), peeled, seeded,
   and cubed
2 small **carrots**, peeled and
   cut into thick batons
½ inch **cinnamon stick**
½ teaspoon **turmeric**
¼ teaspoon **cayenne pepper**
   (optional)
½ teaspoon **ground cumin**
1 teaspoon **paprika**
pinch of **saffron** threads
1 tablespoon **tomato paste**
3 cups hot **vegetable broth**
1 **mango**, peeled, pitted, and
   cut into 1 inch chunks
salt and **black pepper**
2 tablespoons chopped
   cilantro, to garnish

Heat the oil in a large, heavy saucepan over medium heat, add the onion, and sauté for 5 minutes or until beginning to soften. Add the garlic, butternut squash, carrots, and spices and sauté gently for another 5 minutes.

Stir in the tomato paste, then pour in the broth and season with salt and black pepper to taste. Cover and simmer gently for 20–25 minutes or until the vegetables are tender. Stir in the mango and simmer gently for another 5 minutes.

Ladle the tagine into serving bowls, sprinkle with the cilantro, and serve with steamed couscous, if desired.

For spicy squash & carrot soup, make the tagine as above, adding an extra 1 cup vegetable broth. Once the vegetables are tender, put into a blender or food processor and blend until smooth. Ladle into bowls and serve sprinkled with the chopped cilantro. **Calories per serving 237**

eggplant & sweet potato wedges

Calories per serving **238**
Serves **4**
Preparation time **15 minutes**
Cooking time **1 hour**

2 **small-medium eggplants**
   (about 12 oz each)
¼ cup **brown miso paste**
3½ cups **boiling water**
2 tablespoons **sunflower oil**
2 inch piece of **fresh ginger
   root**, grated
2 **garlic cloves**, crushed
3–4 **sweet potatoes** (about
   1¼ lb), cut into wedges
12 **scallions**, thickly sliced
   diagonally
bunch of **parsley**, chopped
salt

Peel the eggplants using a vegetable peeler and coarsely spread the miso paste over the flesh, then put into 2 medium roasting pans. Pour 1 cup of the measured water into each pan, then add 1 tablespoon of the oil, the ginger, and garlic. Sprinkle with salt.

Put the sweet potatoes into a separate roasting pan and drizzle with the remaining oil.

Roast the eggplants and sweet potatoes in a preheated oven, at 350°F, for 30 minutes, then pour ½ cup of the measured water into each eggplant pan and roast for another 20 minutes. Repeat, adding another ¼ cup measured water to each eggplant pan, divide the scallions among them and roast for another 10 minutes, until the eggplants are soft in the center and the sweet potatoes are tender.

Sprinkle the sweet potatoes with the chopped parsley and cut the eggplants into thick "steaks." Serve the eggplants on top of the sweet potatoes with the miso juice from the pans drizzled over the top.

scallops wrapped in prosciutto

Calories per serving **232**
Serves **4**
Preparation time **15 minutes**
Cooking time **4 minutes**

6 slices of **prosciutto**
12 cleaned **sea scallops**,
   corals removed (optional)
4 long **rosemary sprigs**
1 tablespoon **olive oil**
salad greens
salt and **black pepper**

Dressing
¼ cup **lemon juice**, plus extra
   to serve
1 **garlic clove**, crushed
1 tablespoon **white wine
   vinegar**
3 tablespoons **olive oil**
1 teaspoon **Dijon mustard**

Cut the slices of prosciutto in half horizontally. Wrap half a slice around the outside of each scallop.

Thread 3 of the scallops onto a metal skewer, alternating with the corals, if using. Once the holes have been made in each scallop, remove the metal skewers and strip the rosemary sprigs of their leaves, leaving just a tuft at the end. Thread the scallops onto the rosemary skewers.

Season the scallops with only black pepper. Drizzle the scallops with the oil and cook on a hot barbecue grill rack or under a hot boiler for 2 minutes on each side, until cooked through.

Put the dressing ingredients into a bowl and whisk together. Season to taste with salt and black pepper. Use to dress the salad greens and serve with the scallops, seasoned with a squeeze of lemon juice.

For scallop, chorizo & red pepper skewers, thread 1 chopped 10 g slice of chorizo sausage (about ⅜ oz), 1 red bell pepper, cored, seeded, and cut into chunks, and 2 cleaned scallops onto each of 4 presoaked bamboo skewers. Season with salt and black pepper, then place on a hot barbecue grill rack or under a hot broiler for 5 minutes, turning occasionally, until the chorizo and scallops are cooked. Serve with the dressed salad as above. **Calories per serving 238**

onion bhajis

Calories per serving **236**
Serves **4**
Preparation time **10 minutes**
Cooking time **6–8 minutes**

2 **onions**, thinly sliced
1¼ cups **chickpea flour**
2 teaspoons **cumin seeds**
1 teaspoon **ground coriander**
½ teaspoon **turmeric**
1 **green chile,** seeded and
  finely chopped
½ cup **water**
vegetable oil, for frying

Mix together all the ingredients except the water and oil in a bowl. Stir in enough of the measured water to bind the ingredients together and make a thick batter.

Fill a deep saucepan halfway with vegetable oil and heat to 350–375°F, or until a cube of bread browns in 30 seconds. Carefully lower tablespoons of the mixture into the oil, in batches if necessary, and cook for 3–4 minutes, turning until all sides are golden. Remove with a slotted spoon and drain on paper towels.

For onion soup, heat 1 tablespoon olive oil and 4 teaspoons butter in a saucepan, add 6 sliced onions (about 1½ lb), then cover with a piece of wax paper and cook over low heat for 40 minutes, until they are dark; do not let them stick. Pour in ½ cup red wine and bring to a boil. Stir in 2 tablespoons chickpea flour and 6⅓ cups beef broth, season well, and simmer for 30 minutes. **Calories per serving 195**

poached eggs & spinach

Calories per serving **217**
  (not including butter)
Serves **4**
Preparation time **5 minutes**
Cooking time **8–10 minutes**

2 tablespoons **balsamic**
  vinegar
4 strips of **cherry tomatoes**
  on the vine (about
  6 tomatoes on each)
small bunch of **basil**,
  leaves only
1 tablespoon **distilled white**
  vinegar
4 **extra-large eggs**
4 thick slices of **whole-grain**
  bread
3½ cups **baby spinach**
salt and **black pepper**

Pour the balsamic vinegar into a small saucepan and simmer until reduced by half and it forms syrupy glaze. Set aside.

Lay the cherry tomato vines in an ovenproof dish, drizzle with the balsamic glaze, sprinkle with the basil leaves, and season with salt and black pepper. Put into a preheated oven, at 350°F, for 8–10 minutes, or until the tomatoes begin to collapse.

Meanwhile, bring a large saucepan of water to a gentle simmer, add the distilled white vinegar, and stir with a large spoon to create a swirl. Carefully break 2 eggs into the water and cook for 3 minutes. Remove with a slotted spoon and keep warm. Repeat with the remaining eggs.

Toast the bread and butter lightly, if desired.

Pile the spinach onto 4 serving plates and top each plate with a poached egg. Arrange the tomatoes on the plates and drizzle with any cooking juices. Serve immediately with the toast, cut into strips.

For spinach, egg & cress salad, gently lower the unshelled eggs into a saucepan of simmering water. Cook for 7–8 minutes, then cool quickly under cold running water. Mix together 2 tablespoons olive oil and 2 tablespoons balsamic vinegar in a small bowl. Shell the eggs and slice thickly. Arrange the egg slices over the baby spinach leaves and halved cherry tomatoes. Sprinkle with ½ cup garden cress or other microgreens and drizzle with the dressing. Serve immediately. **Calories per serving 210**

white fish with tomato salad

Calories per serving **299**
Serves **4**
Preparation time **15 minutes**
Cooking time **10–12 minutes**

3 tablespoons **olive oil**
¼ cup chopped **cilantro**
2 **garlic cloves**, crushed
1 teaspoon **coriander seeds**,
  crushed
juice of ½ **lemon**
1 **green chile**, seeded and
  finely diced
4 **bream, red snapper**, or
  sea bass fillets (about
  5 oz each)

Tomato salad
1 tablespoon **walnuts**
4 **plum tomatoes**, chopped
1 tablespoon **olive oil**
1 tablespoon chopped
  cilantro

Heat a nonstick skillet over medium-low heat and dry-fry the walnuts for 3–4 minutes, stirring frequently, until golden and toasted. Set aside.

Make the spicy dressing for the fish. Mix together the oil, chopped cilantro, garlic, coriander seeds, lemon juice, and chile in a bowl, then brush the spice mixture over both sides of the fish fillets.

Line a baking sheet with aluminum foil and place the fillets, skin side down, on the foil. Cook under a preheated hot broiler for 3–4 minutes on each side, until cooked through.

Meanwhile, make the tomato salad. Mix together the tomatoes, toasted walnuts, oil, and chopped cilantro in a bowl.

Serve the fish with the tomato salad.

For whole baked white fish, divide 4 chopped garlic cloves, 2 sliced red chiles, 1 trimmed, cleaned, and sliced leek, ¼ cup chopped parsley, and 2 sliced lemons between the cavities of 2 gutted and cleaned whole sea bream, red snappers, or ocean perch. Place in a large baking pan and drizzle with 1 cup white wine and ¼ cup olive oil. Cover with aluminum foil and put into a preheated oven, at 400°F, for 10–15 minutes, until the fish are cooked through. Divide the fish among 4 plates and serve with steamed green vegetables. **Calories per serving 258**

spicy beef with scallions

Calories per serving **213**
Serves **4**
Preparation time **10 minutes**
Cooking time **15 minutes**

3 tablespoons **no-added-sugar oyster sauce**
2 tablespoons **no-added-sugar Chinese rice wine**
2 teaspoons **dried red pepper flakes** or 2 **dried red chiles**, halved
½ cup **beef broth**, cooled
1 teaspoon **honey**
1 tablespoon **cornstarch**
low-calorie **cooking spray**
1 lb lean **sirloin steak**, very thinly sliced
12 **scallions**, diagonally cut into 1½ inch pieces

Mix together the oyster sauce, rice wine, red pepper flakes, broth, honey, and cornstarch in a small bowl until smooth.

Spray a large nonstick wok or skillet with cooking spray and heat over high heat until smoking hot.

Add the steak and stir-fry for 3–4 minutes, until browned and sealed. Stir in the oyster sauce mixture, then add the scallions and continue cooking, stirring frequently, for 10 minutes, or until the steak is tender.

For spicy chicken & vegetable stir-fry, follow the recipe above, replacing the beef with 1 lb chicken breast strips, cut in half lengthwise, and adding 1 small carrot, finely julienned, and 1½ cups snow peas, thinly sliced lengthwise, instead of the scallions. **Calories per serving 202**

harissa chicken with tabbouleh

Calories per serving **281**
Serves **4**
Preparation time **10 minutes**
Cooking time **25–30 minutes**

4 **boneless, skinless chicken breasts** (about 5 oz each)
2 teaspoons **no-added-sugar harissa paste** (for homemade, see page 202)
1 teaspoon **olive oil**
1 teaspoon **dried oregano**
16 **cherry tomatoes** (about 8 oz)
¾ cup **pitted black ripe olives**
½ cup **quinoa**
bunch of **parsley**, chopped
bunch of **cilantro**, chopped
bunch of **mint**, chopped
1 **preserved lemon**, diced

Put the chicken breasts into a roasting pan. Mix together the harissa, oil, and oregano in a bowl, then rub the mixture all over the chicken breasts.

Cover with aluminum foil and roast in a preheated oven, at 400°F, for 15–16 minutes. Remove the foil, add the tomatoes and olives, and return to the oven for another 10–12 minutes, or until the chicken is cooked through.

Meanwhile, cook the quinoa in a saucepan of boiling water according to the package directions, then drain and mix with the chopped herbs and preserved lemon.

Slice the chicken and serve with the tabbouleh, tomatoes, and olives and any juices from the pan.

For harissa chicken soup, heat 1 tablespoon olive oil in a skillet, add 1 chopped onion, 2 peeled and chopped carrots, and 1 chopped garlic clove, and cook for 4–5 minutes, until softened. Stir in 1 tablespoon harissa paste (see page 202) and cook for another 1 minute. Stir in 1⅔ cups canned diced tomatoes, 1⅔ cups rinsed, drained canned chickpeas (garbanzo beans), and 4¼ cups chicken broth. Bring to a boil, then reduce the heat and simmer for 15 minutes. Stir in ⅔ cup shredded cooked chicken and ⅓ cup chopped dried apricots and cook for 10 minutes. Serve sprinkled with 1 tablespoon chopped parsley. **Calories per serving 232**

spicy tofu & vegetable stir-fry

Calories per serving **293**
  (not including rice)
Serves **4**
Preparation time **10 minutes**
Cooking time **6 minutes**

¼ cup **vegetable oil**
6 **scallions**, finely sliced
2 **red chiles**, thinly sliced
1 inch piece of **fresh ginger
  root**, peeled and finely
  chopped
4 **garlic cloves**, finely sliced
1 teaspoon crushed **Sichuan
  peppercorns**
8 oz **firm tofu**, cut into 1 inch
  cubes
3 cups **snow peas**, halved
10 **baby corn**, halved
  lengthwise
3½ cups chopped **bok choy**
3¼ cups **bean sprouts**
2 tablespoons **light soy sauce**
2 tablespoons **no-added-
  sugar Chinese rice wine**
4 teaspoons **sesame oil**
salt

Heat 2 tablespoons of the vegetable oil in a wok or
deep skillet, add the scallions, chiles, ginger, garlic,
peppercorns, and a pinch of salt. Cook for 1 minute,
then add the tofu and stir-fry for another 2 minutes.
Transfer to a plate.

Heat the remaining vegetable oil in the pan and stir-fry
the snow peas, corn, bok choy, and bean sprouts for
a few minutes, until starting to wilt, then add the soy
sauce and rice wine.

Return the tofu mixture to the wok or pan and toss
everything together. Drizzle with the sesame oil and
serve with brown rice, if desired.

thai steamed fish

Calories per serving **213**
Serves **4**
Preparation time **15 minutes**
Cooking time **15 minutes**

4 **trout fillets** (about 5 oz each)
2 inch piece of **fresh ginger
  root**, peeled and chopped
2 **garlic cloves**, chopped
2 **red chiles**, seeded and
  finely chopped
8 **scallions**, sliced
grated zest and juice of
  2 **limes**
4 heads of **baby bok choy**,
  quartered
¼ cup **soy sauce**

Lay 2 pieces of large aluminum foil on a work surface. Place 2 trout fillets on each piece of foil, then divide the ginger, garlic, chiles, scallions, and lime zest between them. Drizzle with the lime juice.

Spread the bok choy around and on top of the fish, then pour the soy sauce on top. Loosely seal the foil to form packages, leaving enough space for steam to circulate as the fish cooks.

Transfer the packages to a steamer and cook for 15 minutes, or until the fish is cooked through.

Open the packages carefully, then serve the fish and bok choy drizzled with the juices.

For Thai fish curry, cook 1 tablespoon no-added-sugar red Thai curry paste in a wok for 1 minute, add 1 sliced onion, and cook for 4–5 minutes, until softened. Pour in 1⅔ cups coconut milk and bring to a boil, then add 1 lb skinless salmon fillets, cut into chunks, and 2 cups trimmed and chopped green beans, reduce the heat, and simmer for 5 minutes, until the fish is cooked and the beans are tender. Sprinkle with 1 tablespoon chopped cilantro and serve with brown rice, if desired. **Calories per serving 448 (not including rice)**

wasabi beef with garlic bok choy

Calories per serving **295**
Serves **4**
Preparation time **10 minutes**
Cooking time **10–12 minutes**

1 tablespoon **sesame seeds**
2 tablespoons **olive oil**
2 teaspoons **no-added-sugar wasabi paste**
4 **tenderloin steaks** (about 5 oz each)
¼ head of **bok choy**, cut lengthwise into 8 pieces
5 **garlic cloves**, finely chopped
½ **red chile,** seeded and finely diced
1 tablespoon **soy sauce**

Heat a nonstick skillet over medium-low heat and dry-fry the sesame seeds for 2 minutes, stirring frequently, until golden brown and toasted. Set aside.

Mix 1 tablespoon of the oil with the wasabi paste in a small bowl, then brush over the steaks.

Heat a ridged grill pan until hot, add the steaks, and cook for 3–4 minutes on each side, depending on how rare you prefer your steak. Let rest for 5 minutes.

Meanwhile, toss the bok choy in the remaining oil with the garlic, chile, and soy sauce, then cook in the ridged grill pan for 2–3 minutes, until wilted.

Slice the steaks, then serve with the bok choy, sprinkled with the toasted sesame seeds.

For beef & bok choy stir-fry, heat 1 tablespoon sunflower oil in a wok or skillet and cook 10 oz sliced tenderloin steak for 3–4 minutes, until browned, then remove from the pan. Add 4 cups broccoli florets, 4 cups sugar snap peas, 4 sliced scallions, 2 chopped garlic cloves, 3 tablespoons peeled and chopped fresh ginger root, 3 quartered heads of baby bok choy, and a splash of water to the pan and stir-fry for 6–7 minutes, until the vegetables soften. Return the beef to the pan and heat through. Serve with a sprinkling of soy sauce. **Calories per serving 203**

piri piri swordfish with tomato salsa

Calories per serving **294**
Serves **4**
Preparation time **10 minutes,
plus marinating**
Cooking time **11–16 minutes**

2 tablespoons **no-added-
sugar piri piri seasoning**
2 tablespoons **olive oil**
4 **swordfish steaks** (about
7 oz each)
6 ripe **plum tomatoes**, halved
1 tablespoon finely chopped
parsley
1 tablespoon finely chopped
basil
1 **green chile,** seeded and
finely chopped
grated zest of **1 lemon,** plus
a little juice
salt and **black pepper**
lemon wedges, to serve

Mix the piri piri seasoning with 1 tablespoon of the oil and rub it over the swordfish steaks. Cover and let marinate in the refrigerator for 30 minutes.

Place the tomatoes on a hot barbecue grill rack or under a hot broiler and cook for 5–8 minutes, until blackened slightly and soft. Let cool slightly, then coarsely chop and transfer to a bowl. Stir in the parsley, basil, chile, and lemon zest. Add a little lemon juice and the remaining oil and season with salt and black pepper.

Cook the marinated swordfish on the grill rack or under the broiler for 3–4 minutes on each side, or until cooked through. Serve with the tomato salsa and lemon wedges.

For barbecued bell pepper relish, to serve as an alternative accompaniment, core, seed, and chop 1 red, 1 yellow, and 1 orange bell pepper into large chunks. Rub the bell peppers with 1 tablespoon olive oil mixed with 1 tablespoon no-added-sugar piri piri seasoning. Place the bell peppers on a hot barbecue grill rack or under a hot broiler and cook until they have blackened slightly and become really soft, then remove, chop the chunks into smaller pieces, and mix with 2 tablespoons olive oil, a little lime juice, 1 tablespoon chopped cilantro, and 1 seeded and finely chopped red chile. Season with salt and black pepper. **Calories per serving 128**

prune & oat loaf

Calories per slice **251**
Makes **10 slices**
Preparation time **10 minutes**
Cooking time **40–45 minutes**

¼ cup grated or finely
   chopped **coconut oil**, plus
   extra for greasing
1¾ cups **pitted prunes**,
   chopped
1 cup **rolled oats**
1½ teaspoons **baking soda**
½ cup **boiling water**
2 **eggs**
⅔ cup **honey**
1½ cups **whole-wheat flour**
¼ teaspoon **ground
   cinnamon**

Grease a 9 x 5 x 3 inch loaf pan with coconut oil and
line the bottom with nonstick parchment paper.

Put the prunes, oats, baking soda, and coconut oil into
a heatproof bowl, pour over the measured water, and
let stand.

Meanwhile, whisk together the eggs and honey in
a separate bowl until well combined, then fold in the
flour and cinnamon. Add the prune and oat mixture
and mix well.

Spoon the batter into the prepared pan and bake
in a preheated oven, at 350°F, for 40–45 minutes,
until a toothpick inserted in the center comes out clean.
Cover the top with aluminum foil if it starts to brown
too quickly.

Turn out onto a wire rack and let cool before cutting
into 10 slices to serve.

For prune & cinnamon oatmeal, put 2⅓ cups rolled
oats, ⅔ cup chopped pitted prunes, ¼ teaspoon ground
cinnamon, 1 tablespoon coconut oil, and 6⅓ cups
milk or water into a saucepan and bring to a boil, then
reduce the heat and simmer for 4–5 minutes, stirring
occasionally, until thick and creamy. To serve, pour into
6 bowls and drizzle each with 1 tablespoon honey.
Calories per serving 373

cheesy herbed muffins

Calories per muffin **281**
Makes **8**
Preparation time **5 minutes**
Cooking time **20 minutes**

1½ cups shredded **Gruyère cheese**
3 **scallions**, finely sliced
1 teaspoon **thyme leaves**
1 tablespoon chopped **parsley**
⅔ cup **rice flour**
½ teaspoon **gluten-free baking powder**
3 cups **fresh gluten-free bread crumbs**
1 teaspoon **no-added-sugar English mustard**
3 **eggs**, beaten
3½ tablespoons **butter**, melted
¼ cup **milk**

Line 8 cups of a muffin pan with paper muffin liners.

Mix together all the ingredients in a large bowl until just combined and spoon the batter into the muffin liners.

Put into a preheated oven, at 375°F, for 20 minutes, or until golden and just firm to the touch. Remove from the oven and serve warm.

brazil chocolate brownies

Calories per brownie **289**
Makes **12**
Preparation time **10 minutes,
  plus cooling**
Cooking time **40–45 minutes**

½ cup **coconut oil**, plus extra
  for greasing
4 oz **dark no-added-sugar
  chocolate**, broken into
  pieces
½ cup **milk**
¾ cup **honey**
½ cup plus 1 tablespoon
  **unsweetened cocoa
  powder**
3 **eggs**
1⅓ cups **spelt flour**
1 teaspoon **baking powder**
¼ cup coarsely chopped
  Brazil nuts

Grease a 7 x 7 inch baking pan and line with nonstick
parchment paper.

Put the coconut oil, chocolate, milk and honey into
a saucepan and heat gently, stirring, until melted.
Remove from the heat and stir in the cocoa powder,
then let cool for a few minutes.

Beat in the eggs, then fold in the flour, baking powder,
and Brazil nuts. Pour the mixture into the prepared pan.

Bake in a preheated oven, at 375°F, for 35–40 minutes,
until just set. Let cool in the pan for 15 minutes, then
transfer to a wire rack and let cool completely. Cut into
12 squares to serve.

For chocolate avocado mousse, put the flesh of
2 large avocados, 2 tablespoons unsweetened cocoa
powder, 3 tablespoons maple syrup, and 2 tablespoons
coconut cream (from the top of a can of coconut milk)
in a food processor or blender and blend until smooth.
Add 5 oz melted dark no-added-sugar chocolate and
blend again. Spoon into 4 small bowls or glasses and
serve with fresh raspberries. **Calories per serving 434**

summer smoothie

Calories per serving **276**
Serves **1**
Preparation time **5 minutes,**
  plus soaking

1 tablespoon **goji berries**
3 **pitted dates**
2 tablespoons **almond milk**
¾ cup **raspberries**, plus extra
  to decorate
½ cup halved hulled
  strawberries
1 tablespoon **honey**
3 tablespoons **plain yogurt**
½ cup **coconut water**

Put the goji berries and dates into a bowl, pour
the almond milk over the fruit, and let soak in the
refrigerator for 3 hours, or preferably overnight.

Transfer the goji berry mixture to a blender or food
processor, add all the remaining ingredients, and blend
until smooth, adding a little more coconut water to
loosen, if needed.

Pour into a glass, decorate with a few extra raspberries,
and serve.

For summer fruit dessert, toss together ½ cup
hulled and halved strawberries, ⅓ cup raspberries,
⅓ cup blueberries, and 2 tablespoons chopped mint in
a serving bowl. Serve with 3 tablespoons plain yogurt.
Calories per serving 90

tropical fruit desserts

Calories per serving **280**
Serves **4**
Preparation time **15 minutes**

4 **bananas**, sliced
grated zest and juice of
  1 **orange**
3 cups **plain yogurt**
2 **mangoes**, peeled, pitted,
  and chopped
6 **passion fruit**, halved

Put the bananas into a large bowl and toss with the orange zest and juice. Spoon into 4 glasses or bowls.

Top with half the yogurt, then add the mango chunks. Divide the remaining yogurt evenly among the glasses.

Spoon the pulp of the passion fruit on top and serve.

For baked bananas, bake 4 unpeeled bananas in a preheated oven, at 400°F, for 30 minutes, until the skins are black. Halve lengthwise and top each one with 1 tablespoon plain yogurt, 1 tablespoon chopped pistachios, and a drizzle of honey. **Calories per serving 250**

crepes with fruit compote

Calories per serving **268**
Serves **4**
Preparation time **10 minutes,
  plus chilling**
Cooking time **20 minutes**

¾ cup plus 1 tablespoon
  buckwheat flour, sifted
½ teaspoon **ground
  cinnamon**
1 **extra-large egg**, beaten
⅔ cup **milk**
2 teaspoons **vegetable oil**
¼ cup **plain yogurt**, to serve

Compote
2 **sweet, crisp apples**, peeled,
  cored, and chopped
2 **pears**, peeled, cored, and
  chopped
⅔ cup **blueberries**
grated zest and juice of
  1 **orange**
2–3 tablespoons **water**

Put the flour and half the cinnamon into a bowl and make a well in the center. Gradually whisk in the egg and milk to form a smooth batter. Chill for 30 minutes.

Heat a little of the oil in a skillet and pour a ladleful of the batter into the pan, swirling it around to cover the bottom. Cook until bubbles appear on the surface, then loosen the edges and turn over with a spatula and cook for another 1 minute, until golden. Remove from the pan and keep warm. Repeat with the remaining oil and batter to make 8 pancakes.

Meanwhile, make the fruit compote. Put all the ingredients into a small saucepan and simmer for 10 minutes, until softened. Keep warm.

Serve the pancakes with the fruit compote, topped with yogurt and sprinkled with the remaining cinnamon.

For cinnamon fruit salad, mix together 2 peeled, cored, and chopped sweet, crisp apples and 2 peeled, cored, and chopped pears in a bowl with ⅔ cup blueberries, 1 peeled, pitted, and chopped mango, and 2 peeled and sliced kiwifruit. Pour the juice of 2 oranges over the fruit, sprinkle with 1 teaspoon ground cinnamon, and toss together. Let stand for 20–30 minutes. Spoon into 4 bowls and serve each with 1 tablespoon plain yogurt. **Calories per serving 168**

green fruit salad

Calories per serving **262**
Serves **6**
Preparation time **15 minutes**

2 cups **seedless green
  grapes**, halved
4 **kiwifruit**, peeled, quartered,
  and sliced
2 ripe **pears**, peeled, cored,
  and sliced
4 **passion fruit**, halved
¼ cup **no-added-sugar
  elderflower syrup** or
  other **fruit syrup**
¼ cup **water**
1¼ cups **Greek yogurt**
2 tablespoons **honey**

Put the grapes, kiwifruit, and pears into a bowl. Using
a teaspoon, scoop the seeds from 3 of the passion fruit
into the bowl. Mix 2 tablespoons of the syrup with the
measured water and drizzle it over the salad. Gently toss
together and spoon into 6 glasses.

Stir the remaining undiluted syrup into the yogurt, then
mix in the honey. Spoon into the glasses. Decorate with
the remaining passion fruit seeds and serve.

For ruby fruit salad, mix 2 cups halved seedless red
grapes with 1¼ cups fresh raspberries and 1 cup
sliced, hulled strawberries. Sprinkle with the seeds from
½ pomegranate, then drizzle with ⅓ cup no-added-
sugar red grape juice. Mix the yogurt with only honey,
then spoon it over the fruit salad. Decorate with a few
extra pomegranate seeds. **Calories per serving 209**

116

baked stuffed pears

Calories per serving **217**
Serves **4**
Preparation time **10 minutes**
Cooking time **35–40 minutes**

4 **pears**, halved and cored
²/₃ cup chopped **pitted dates**
1 tablespoon **sesame seeds**
½ teaspoon **ground
   cinnamon**
2 tablespoons **maple syrup**
grated zest and juice of
   1 orange
¼ cup **plain yogurt**

Put one half of each of the pears into an ovenproof dish and sprinkle each one with the dates, sesame seeds, cinnamon, maple syrup, and orange juice.

Top with the remaining pear halves, cover the dish with aluminum foil, and bake in a preheated oven, at 350°F, for 35–40 minutes, until the pears are tender.

Stir together the orange zest and yogurt in a small bowl, then serve with the baked pears.

For baked chocolate pears, halve 4 pears, scoop out the cores, and put into a baking pan. Sprinkle each half with ¼ tablespoon cocoa nibs, ½ teaspoon honey, and 1 teaspoon ground almonds (almond meal). Squeeze the juice of 1 orange over the top, cover with aluminum foil, and cook as above for 30 minutes, or until tender. **Calories per serving 267**

less than
400 calories

butternut & prosciutto salad

Calories per serving **372**
Serves **4**
Preparation time **10 minutes**
Cooking time **27 minutes**

1 **butternut squash** (about
  2 lb), peeled, seeded, and
  cut into chunks
2 **red onions**, cut into wedges
2 tablespoons **pumpkin
  seeds**
1 tablespoon **olive oil**
6 oz **asparagus tips**
12 slices of **prosciutto**
2 tablespoons **extra virgin
  olive oil**
1 tablespoon **balsamic
  vinegar**
2 heads of **endive**,
  leaves separated
salt and **black pepper**

Put the butternut squash and onions into a roasting
pan, sprinkle in the pumpkin seeds, and toss with the
olive oil and some salt and black pepper.

Roast in a preheated oven, at 400°F, for 22 minutes,
until starting to caramelize, then toss in the asparagus
tips and roast for another 5 minutes.

Meanwhile, put the prosciutto under a preheated hot
broiler for 4–5 minutes, until crisp.

Make the dressing. Whisk together the extra virgin olive
oil and vinegar in a small bowl.

Divide the endive leaves among 4 plates and top with
the roasted vegetables and prosciutto. Drizzle with the
dressing and serve.

grilled summer chicken salad

Calories per serving **365**
Serves **4**
Preparation time **15 minutes**
Cooking time **40–45 minutes**

4 **boneless, skinless chicken breasts** (about 4 oz each)
2 small **red onions**
2 **red bell peppers**, cored, seeded, and cut into flat pieces
16 **asparagus spears** (about 5 oz), trimmed
7 oz **cooked new potatoes**, halved
bunch of **basil**
⅓ cup **olive oil**
2 tablespoons **balsamic vinegar**
salt and **black pepper**

Heat a ridged grill pan or skillet, add the chicken breasts, and cook for 8–10 minutes on each side until cooked through. Remove from the pan and cut into chunks.

Cut the red onions into wedges, keeping the root ends intact to hold the wedges together. Place in the pan and cook for 5 minutes on each side. Remove from the pan and set aside.

Place the flat pieces of red bell pepper in the pan and cook for 8 minutes on only the skin side, so that the skins are charred and blistered. Remove and set aside, then cook the asparagus in the pan for 6 minutes, turning frequently.

Put the cooked potatoes into a large bowl. Tear the basil, reserving a few leaves for garnish, and add to the bowl, together with the chicken and all the vegetables. Add the olive oil, balsamic vinegar, and seasoning. Toss the salad and garnish with the reserved basil leaves.

For summer chicken wraps, omit the potatoes and make the recipe as above. Warm 4 soft whole-wheat tortillas as directed on the package, then spread with ¾ cup reduced-fat hummus. Toss the grilled chicken, cut into strips, and vegetables with 2 tablespoons olive oil, the balsamic vinegar as above, and reserved basil leaves. Divide among the tortillas, then roll up tightly and serve cut in half while the chicken is still warm. **Calories per serving 499**

corn, tomato & black bean salad

Calories per serving **370**
Serves **4**
Preparation time **10 minutes**
Cooking time **10 minutes**

4 **corn cobs**, shucked
16 **cherry tomatoes**
  (about 8 oz), halved
1 ½ cups rinsed, drained
  canned **black beans**
1 **red onion**, finely diced
1 **avocado**, peeled, pitted,
  and diced
small bunch of **cilantro**,
  coarsely chopped
juice of **1 lime**
2 tablespoons **canola oil**
2–3 drops of **Tabasco sauce**

Cook the corn cobs in a saucepan of boiling water for 7–10 minutes. Cool briefly under cold running water, then scrape off the kernels with a knife.

Put the kernels into a large bowl with the tomatoes, black beans, onion, and avocado and mix together with the cilantro.

Whisk together the lime juice, oil, and Tabasco in a small bowl.

Drizzle the dressing over the salad, stir carefully to combine, and serve immediately.

For spicy shrimp with corn & black bean salad,

make the salad as above. Heat 1 ½ tablespoons vegetable oil in a wok or large skillet over high heat, add 24 peeled and butterflied shrimp with the tails on, and stir-fry for 1 minute, then add 2 finely chopped garlic cloves and 2 seeded and finely chopped long red chiles. Cook for another 2 minutes, until the shrimp turn pink and are just cooked through. Stir through 3 tablespoons chopped cilantro. Serve the shrimp on the salad, garnished with extra cilantro leaves and lime wedges. **Calories per serving 464**

roasted beet soup

Calories per serving **360**
Serves **4**
Preparation time **15 minutes**
Cooking time **1 hour**
  5 minutes

7 **raw beets** (about 1 ¼ lb)
4 **Yukon gold** or **white round**
  potatoes (about 1 lb),
  peeled and chopped
1 tablespoon **pumpkin seeds**
1 ²/₃ cups **coconut milk**
juice of 1 **lemon**
2 teaspoons **ground**
  coriander
2 teaspoons **dried red**
  pepper flakes
1 teaspoon **ground cumin**
1 **garlic clove**, crushed
salt and **black pepper**
2 tablespoons **plain yogurt**,
  to serve

Put the beets into a roasting pan and roast in a preheated oven, at 400°F, for 1 hour, until tender. Let cool slightly, then peel off the skins.

Meanwhile, cook the potatoes in a saucepan of boiling water for 15–18 minutes, until tender.

Heat a nonstick skillet over medium-low heat and dry-fry the pumpkin seeds for 2–3 minutes, stirring frequently, until slightly golden and toasted. Set aside.

Transfer the beets and potatoes to a blender with the remaining ingredients and blend until smooth. Pour the soup into a saucepan, season to taste, and heat through.

Ladle into 4 bowls, sprinkle with the toasted seeds, and serve with dollops of yogurt.

For roasted beet salad, peel 4 raw beets and cut into wedges. Put into a roasting pan with 1 large red onion, cut into wedges, and sprinkle with 1 teaspoon cumin seeds and 1 tablespoon olive oil. Roast as above for 45–50 minutes, until the beets are tender. Toss together ½ bunch of watercress or 2 cups other peppery greens, 1 cup arugula leaves, and ⅓ cup shredded red cabbage in a serving bowl. Add the beets, onion, 2 tablespoons extra virgin olive oil, and the juice of ½ lemon. Season and toss together. Serve sprinkled with 1 ¼ cups grated Manchego cheese and 1 tablespoon chopped cilantro. **Calories per serving 252**

beery oxtail & lima bean soup

Calories per serving **310**
Serves **6**
Preparation time **25 minutes**
Cooking time **4¼ hours**

1 tablespoon **sunflower oil**
1 lb **oxtail pieces**, string
   removed, or **beef shank**
1 **onion**, finely chopped
2 **carrots**, peeled and diced
2 **celery sticks**, diced
2 **Yukon gold** or **white round**
   potatoes, peeled and diced
small bunch of **mixed herbs**
8½ cups **beef broth**
2 cups **strong ale**
2 teaspoons **no-added-sugar**
   English mustard
1 tablespoon **tomato paste**
1⅔ cups drained canned
   lima beans
salt and **black pepper**
chopped **parsley**, to garnish

Heat the oil in a large saucepan, add the oxtail pieces, and cooked until browned on one side. Turn the oxtail pieces over and add the onion, stirring until browned on all sides. Stir in the carrots, celery, potatoes, and herbs and cook for another 2–3 minutes.

Pour in the broth and ale, then add the mustard, tomato paste, and lima beans. Season well with salt and black pepper and bring to a boil, stirring. Cover the pan halfway with a lid and simmer gently for 4 hours.

Lift the oxtail and herbs out of the pan with a slotted spoon. Discard the herbs and cut the meat off the oxtail bones, discarding any fat. Return the meat to the pan and reheat, then taste and adjust the seasoning, if needed. Ladle into 6 bowls, sprinkle with chopped parsley and serve.

For spicy oxtail & red bean soup, omit the bunch of mixed herbs and instead stir 2 finely chopped garlic cloves, 2 bay leaves, 1 teaspoon hot chili powder, 1 teaspoon crushed cumin seeds, and 1 teaspoon crushed coriander seeds into the vegetables. Add the beef broth, 1⅔ cups canned diced tomatoes, 1 tablespoon tomato paste, and 1⅔ cups rinsed, drained canned red kidney beans. Bring to a boil, simmer, and finish as above. **Calories per serving 298**

herbed smoked salmon omelets

Calories per serving **311**
  (not including baby greens
  and herb salad)
Serves **4**
Preparation time **10 minutes**
Cooking time **15 minutes**

8 **extra-large eggs**
2 **scallions**, thinly sliced
2 tablespoons chopped
  chives
2 tablespoons chopped
  chervil
3½ tablespoons **butter**
4 thin slices of **smoked
  salmon**, cut into thin strips,
  or 4 oz **smoked salmon
  scraps**
black pepper
baby greens and herb salad,
  to serve

Put the eggs, scallions, and herbs into a bowl, beat together lightly, and season with black pepper.

Heat a medium skillet over medium-low heat, add one-quarter of the butter, and melt until beginning to froth. Pour in one-quarter of the egg mixture and swirl to cover the bottom of the pan. Stir gently for 2–3 minutes or until almost set.

Sprinkle with one-quarter of the smoked salmon strips and cook for another 30 seconds, or until just set. Fold over and slide onto a serving plate. Repeat to make another 3 omelets. Serve each omelet immediately with a baby greens and herb salad.

For smoked ham & tomato omelet, make as above, adding 8–12 quartered cherry tomatoes to the egg mixture. Replace the smoked salmon with 4 thin slices of smoked ham, cut into strips. **Calories per serving 295**

beef & bok choy stir-fry

Calories per serving **305**
Serves **4**
Preparation time **15 minutes**
Cooking time **5 minutes**

1 lb **sirloin steak**, trimmed
and cut into strips
1 teaspoon **Chinese five-
spice powder**
2 tablespoons **coconut oil**
1 **red chile,** seeded and
chopped
1 **garlic clove**, chopped
2 inch piece of **fresh ginger
root**, peeled and cut into
matchsticks
1 **lemon grass stalk**, trimmed
and sliced
100 g (3½ oz) **sugar snap peas**
8 **baby corn**, sliced diagonally
6 **scallions**, sliced
2 heads of **baby bok choys**,
coarsely chopped
juice of ½ **lime**
2 tablespoons **soy sauce**
1 tablespoon **no-added-sugar
Thai fish sauce**

To garnish
2 tablespoons **roasted peanuts**
2 tablespoons coarsely
chopped **cilantro**

Toss together the beef strips and five-spice powder
in a bowl, then set aside.

Meanwhile, heat the coconut oil in a wok or large
skillet, add the chile, garlic, ginger, and lemon grass and
cook for 1 minute, until softened. Remove with a slotted
spoon and set aside.

Add the beef to the pan and cook over high heat for
1 minute, until browned and just cooked through. Return
the chile mixture to the pan with the sugar snaps, baby
corn, and scallions and stir-fry for 1 minute, then add
the bok choy and cook for another 1 minute.

Pour in the lime juice, soy sauce, and fish sauce and
toss well. Spoon onto 4 plates or bowls and serve
sprinkled with the peanuts and chopped cilantro.

For Chinese braised beef, heat 2 tablespoons
sunflower oil in a skillet, add 1¾ lb chopped beef brisket,
and cook until browned. Set aside. Meanwhile, put 2
large chopped onions, ½ cup peeled, coarsely chopped
fresh ginger root, 2 garlic cloves, and the stems of a
small bunch of cilantro in a food processor or blender and
process to a paste. Transfer to a flameproof casserole,
add 1 tablespoon water, and cook for 2 minutes. Stir in
2 teaspoons Chinese five-spice powder, 4 star anise, and
1 teaspoon black peppercorns and cook for 1 minute. Stir
in 2 tablespoons soy sauce, 2 tablespoons tomato paste,
and 2 tablespoons maple syrup, add the beef, pour over
enough water to cover, and bring to a simmer. Cover and
put into a preheated oven, at 325°F, for 2 hours. Serve
with steamed bok choy. **Calories per serving 226**

crusted salmon with tomato salsa

Calories per serving **353**
Serves **4**
Preparation time **10 minutes**
Cooking time **12–15 minutes**

1 tablespoon chopped
  fresh herbs
1 **garlic clove**, crushed
3 tablespoons **cornmeal**
4 skinless **salmon fillets**
  (about 4 oz each)
black pepper

Salsa
2 cups quartered
  cherry tomatoes
1 small **red onion**, finely sliced
½ **red chile,** seeded and finely
  chopped
handful of **cilantro**, chopped

To serve
¼ cup **light crème fraîche**
  or **plain Greek yogurt**
salad greens

Mix together the herbs, garlic, and cornmeal in a shallow bowl. Coat the salmon pieces in the cornmeal mix, pressing it down firmly.

Put the coated fish onto a baking sheet and put into a preheated oven, at 400°F, for 12–15 minutes, until cooked through.

Mix together the salsa ingredients in a bowl. Place the salmon on 4 serving plates, top with the salsa, season with black pepper, and serve with a spoonful of crème fraîche and salad greens.

For cornmeal-crusted chicken, beat together 2 tablespoons cream cheese with the chopped fresh herbs and 1 finely diced garlic clove. Make a horizontal slit in 4 boneless, skinless chicken breasts (about 4 oz each). Fill the cavities of the chicken breasts with the cream cheese mixture, then secure with toothpicks. Dip the chicken breasts in a little gluten-free flour, a little beaten egg, then in the polenta. Cook each chicken breast in 1 tablespoon olive oil for 2–3 minutes on each side, transfer to a baking sheet, and put into a preheated oven, at 400°F, for 10–12 minutes, or until the chicken is cooked through. Serve with the salsa and salad greens. **Calories per serving 362**

mixed bean & tomato chili

Calories per serving **377**
Serves **4**
Preparation time **5 minutes**
Cooking time **20–25 minutes**

2 tablespoons **olive oil**
1 **onion**, finely chopped
4 **garlic cloves**, crushed
1 teaspoon **dried red**
  pepper flakes
2 teaspoons **ground cumin**
1 teaspoon **ground cinnamon**
1 2/3 cups canned **diced**
  tomatoes
1 cup **vegetable broth**
1 2/3 cups rinsed, drained
  canned **mixed beans**,
  such as kidney beans, pinto
  beans, and chickpeas
1 2/3 cups rinsed, drained
  canned **red kidney beans**
salt and **black pepper**

To serve
1/4 cup **sour cream**
1/2 cup finely chopped **cilantro**
4 grilled **corn tortillas**

Heat the oil in a heavy saucepan, add the onion and garlic, and sauté for 3–4 minutes, until softened, then add the red pepper flakes, cumin, and cinnamon. Cook, stirring, for 2–3 minutes.

Stir in the tomatoes and broth and bring to a boil, then reduce the heat to medium and simmer gently for 10 minutes. Add the beans and cook for 3–4 minutes, until warmed through. Season well.

Ladle into 4 bowls and top each with 1 tablespoon of sour cream. Sprinkle with chopped cilantro and serve immediately with the corn tortillas.

For mixed bean & tomato bruschettas, put 1/2 onion, 2 crushed garlic cloves, 1 teaspoon dried red pepper flakes, 1/3 cup canned diced tomatoes, 1 2/3 cups rinsed, drained canned mixed beans, such as red kidney beans, pinto beans, and chickpeas, and 1/4 cup chopped flat leaf parsley in a blender or food processor and process until fairly smooth. Season, then spread the mixture onto 2 halved and toasted ciabatta rolls, drizzle each with 2 teaspoons olive oil, and serve. **Calories per serving 259**

spiced yogurt chicken

Calories per serving **319**
Serves **4**
Preparation time **10 minutes,**
  plus marinating
Cooking time **30–35 minutes**

1 cup **plain yogurt**
juice of **1 lemon**
2 **garlic cloves**, crushed
1 tablespoon peeled and
  grated **fresh ginger root**
1 **green chile,** seeded and
  finely diced
1 teaspoon **turmeric**
1 teaspoon **paprika**
1 teaspoon **garam masala**
2 tablespoons **olive oil**
4 **boneless, skinless chicken**
  breasts (about 5 oz each)
6 **scallions,** sliced
1 (10 oz) package
  fresh spinach
black pepper
2 tablespoons chopped
  cilantro, to garnish
2 tablespoons **toasted**
  slivered almonds, to serve

Mix together the yogurt, lemon juice, garlic, ginger, chile, spices, and 1 tablespoon of the oil in a nonreactive dish. Make a few cuts across the chicken, then place in the marinade, rubbing the mixture into the cuts. Cover and let marinate in the refrigerator for 1 hour.

Put the chicken into a baking pan and bake in a preheated oven, at 400°F, for 30–35 minutes, until golden and cooked through.

Meanwhile, heat the remaining oil in a saucepan, add the scallions, and sauté for 3–4 minutes, until softened, then add the spinach and toss in the hot oil to wilt. Season with black pepper.

Divide the spinach among 4 plates and top each with a chicken breast. Serve sprinkled with the chopped cilantro and slivered almonds.

For spicy chicken open sandwiches, mix together 3 tablespoons no-added-sugar mayonnaise, the juice of ½ lemon, and ½ teaspoon smoked paprika in a bowl. Add 2 cups shredded cooked chicken and 4 sliced scallions. Toast 4 thick slices of gluten-free bread, then top each one with 2 butterhead lettuce leaves and spoon the chicken mixture on top. Peel, pit, and slice 1 mango and serve a few slices on the top of each sandwich, with a sprinkling of cilantro leaves. **Calories per serving 201**

seared tuna with lime crust

Calories per serving **310**
Serves **4**
Preparation time **10 minutes,
  plus marinating**
Cooking time **5 minutes**

4 **tuna steaks** (about
  5 oz each)
2 tablespoons grated
  lime zest
juice of **3 limes**
3 tablespoons chopped **dill**
2 tablespoons chopped
  parsley
1 **red chile,** seeded and
  finely diced
3 tablespoons **olive oil**
6 heads of **baby bok choy,**
  quartered lengthwise
salt and **black pepper**

Put the tuna into a shallow nonreactive dish. Combine the lime zest, juice, dill, parsley, chile, 2 tablespoons of the oil, and salt and black pepper in a small bowl, then pour over the tuna. Cover and let marinate in the refrigerator for 20 minutes, turning the tuna once.

Remove the tuna from the marinade. Heat the remaining oil in a skillet or ridged grill pan and cook the tuna for 1–2 minutes on each side, until just seared. Remove from the pan and thickly slice. Pour any remaining marinade into the pan and bring to a boil.

Meanwhile, put the bok choy into a steamer and cook for 3–4 minutes, until tender.

Divide the bok choy among 4 plates and top with the sliced tuna. Serve drizzled with the hot marinade.

For tuna salad with lime dressing, whisk together 3 tablespoons olive oil, the juice of 1 lime, 1 teaspoon honey, and ½ teaspoon Dijon mustard in a small bowl. Cook 11½ oz tuna steak on a ridged grill pan for 2–3 minutes on each side, then slice. Toss together the leaves of 4 small butterhead lettuce, 12 halved cherry tomatoes, ½ cup black ripe olives, a few sprigs of dill and parsley, and ½ thinly sliced red onion. Toss in the tuna and dressing and serve. **Calories per serving 249**

roasted fennel pork chops

Calories per serving **396**
Serves **4**
Preparation time **10 minutes**
Cooking time **20 minutes**

4 **pork chops** (about
   6 oz each)
1 tablespoon **olive oil**
1 teaspoon **fennel seeds**
2 tablespoons **extra virgin
   olive oil**
2 tablespoons **red wine
   vinegar**
2–3 **sage leaves**, chopped
4 **sweet, crisp apples**, cored
   and thinly sliced into rings
3 **celery sticks**, thickly sliced
12 **green grapes**, halved
black pepper

Brush the chops with the olive oil and sprinkle with the fennel seeds and black pepper.

Place on a rack over a roasting pan and bake in a preheated oven, at 400°F, for 20 minutes, until cooked through.

Meanwhile, whisk together the extra virgin olive oil, vinegar and sage in a bowl.

Toss the apples, celery, and grapes together with the dressing and serve with the roasted chops.

coconut fish curry

Calories per serving **399**
Serves **4**
Preparation time **5 minutes**
Cooking time **12–15 minutes**

1 tablespoon **peanut oil**
2 teaspoons **ground cumin**
2 teaspoons **ground coriander**
2 **green chiles**, seeded and sliced
1 **cinnamon stick**
1 **star anise**
6 **kaffir lime leaves**
1²/₃ cups **light coconut milk**
4 skinless **cod loins** (about 5 oz each)
juice of 1 **lime**
fresh **cilantro leaves**, to garnish (optional)
3 cups cooked **brown long-grain rice**, to serve

Heat the oil in a saucepan, add the spices and lime leaves, and cook, stirring, for 2 minutes, until fragrant. Pour in the coconut milk and simmer for 5 minutes.

Add the fish and simmer for 4–6 minutes, until the fish is tender and cooked through. Stir in the lime juice.

Sprinkle with cilantro leaves, if desired, and serve with the long-grain rice.

For coconut fish soup, bring 4¼ cups fish broth to a simmer in a saucepan, then add ¾ cup chopped kale, ¾ cup sliced mushrooms, 1 sliced red chile, 11½ oz sliced cod loin, and 2 oz peeled shrimp. Simmer for 2–3 minutes, then add 1 cup coconut cream (from the top of canned coconut milk) and simmer for another 4–5 minutes, until the shrimp turn pink and the fish is cooked through. Serve sprinkled with cilantro leaves. **Calories per serving 174**

lamb with eggplant dressing

Calories per serving **348**
Serves **4**
Preparation time **5 minutes,**
   plus marinating
Cooking time **18–20 minutes**

12 **lamb cutlets** (about
   3½ oz each)
1 tablespoon **olive oil**
2 **garlic cloves**, crushed
1 teaspoon **sumac** or
   ground cumin
½ teaspoon **dried oregano**
1 **eggplant**
⅓ cup crumbled **feta cheese**
⅓ cup **plain yogurt**
1 tablespoon **tahini**
juice of 1 **lemon**
½ bunch of **watercress** or
   2 cups other **peppery**
   greens

Put the lamb cutlets into a bowl with half the oil and garlic, the sumac or cumin, and oregano and mix well to coat. Cover and let marinate in the refrigerator for 30 minutes.

Meanwhile, cook the eggplant under a preheated hot broiler for 10 minutes, turning frequently, until the skin is blackened. Let cool, then remove the stalk.

Put the whole eggplant, feta, yogurt, tahini, and lemon juice into a food processor or blender and blend until smooth.

Cook the lamb cutlets under a preheated broiler for 4–5 minutes on each side, depending on how pink you prefer your lamb.

Serve the lamb on a bed of watercress with the eggplant dressing.

For spiced lamb burgers, mix together 1½ lb ground lamb, 2 chopped garlic cloves, 1 tablespoon chopped mint, and 1 teaspoon smoked paprika in a bowl. Shape into 4 burgers, then brush with 1½ teaspoons oil and cook under a preheated hot broiler or on a barbecue grill rack for 5–6 minutes on each side, until cooked through. Serve on a bed of ½ bunch of watercress or 2 cups other peppery greens, 2 cups spinach, and ¼ sliced cucumber dressed with 2 tablespoons no-added-sugar salad dressing. Sprinkle with ⅓ cup crumbled feta cheese to serve. **Calories per serving 458**

spiced mackerel fillets

Calories per serving **399**
  **(not including arugula
  salad)**
Serves **4**
Preparation time **15 minutes**
Cooking time **5–6 minutes**

2 tablespoons **olive oil**
1 tablespoon **smoked paprika**
1 teaspoon **cayenne pepper**
4 **mackerel**, scaled, filleted,
  and pin-boned
2 **limes**, quartered
salt and **black pepper**
arugula salad (optional)

Mix together the oil, paprika, and cayenne with a little salt and black pepper. Make 3 shallow cuts in the skin of the mackerel and brush with the spiced oil.

Place the lime quarters and mackerel onto a hot barbecue grill rack or under a preheated hot broiler, skin side down, and cook for 4–5 minutes, until the skin is crispy and the limes are charred. Turn the fish over and cook for another 1 minute, until cooked through. Serve with a arugula salad, if desired.

For mackerel with black pepper & bay, mix together 4 finely shredded bay leaves, 1 crushed garlic clove, ½ teaspoon black pepper, a pinch of salt, and ¼ cup olive oil. Rub the marinade over and into the cavity of 4 cleaned mackerel. Place them on a hot barbecue grill rack or under a preheated hot broiler and cook for 3–4 minutes on each side. **Calories per serving 445**

bean, chorizo & spinach stew

Calories per serving **318**
Serves **4**
Preparation time **5 minutes**
Cooking time **25 minutes**

1½ teaspoons **olive oil**
4 oz **chorizo**, diced
1 **onion**, chopped
2 **garlic cloves**, chopped
3¼ cups rinsed, drained
  canned **lima beans**
1⅔ cups canned **diced
  tomatoes**
2½ cups **chicken broth**
7 cups **baby spinach leaves**
2 tablespoons chopped
  parsley
salt and **black pepper**

Heat the oil in a large saucepan, add the chorizo, and cook for 2–3 minutes. Add the onion and cook over low heat for another 10 minutes, until soft, then stir in the garlic and cook for another 1 minute.

Add the lima beans, tomatoes, and broth, bring to a gentle simmer, cover, and cook for 10 minutes.

Stir in the spinach and half the parsley and cook for 1 minute, until the spinach has wilted. Season to taste and serve sprinkled with the remaining parsley.

For lima bean dip, put 1⅔ cups canned lima beans, 2 garlic cloves, the juice of 1 lemon, 2 tablespoons olive oil, 1 teaspoon ground cumin, and ½ teaspoon paprika in a food processor or blender and blend until smooth, adding a little water to loosen, if necessary. Serve with chopped vegetables. **Calories per serving 107 (not including vegetables)**

snapper with carrots & caraway

Calories per serving **352**
Serves **4**
Preparation time **10 minutes**
Cooking time **15 minutes**

4 cups sliced **carrots**
  (about 1 lb)
2 teaspoons **caraway seeds**
4 **snapper fillets** (about
  6 oz each), pin-boned
2 **oranges**
bunch of **cilantro**, coarsely
  chopped, plus extra to
  garnish
¼ cup **olive oil**
salt and **black pepper**

Heat a ridged grill pan over medium heat and cook the carrots for 3 minutes on each side, adding the caraway seeds for the last 2 minutes of cooking. Transfer to a bowl and keep warm.

Cook the snapper fillets in the grill pan for 3 minutes on each side, until cooked through. Meanwhile, juice 1 of the oranges and cut the other into quarters. Cook the orange quarters in the pan until browned.

Add the cilantro to the carrots and mix well. Season to taste with salt and black pepper and stir in the oil and orange juice. Serve the cooked fish with the carrots and orange quarters. Garnish with extra cilantro.

For carrot & cilantro puree, to serve as an alternative accompaniment, cook 4 cups peeled and coarsely chopped carrots (about 1 lb) in a saucepan of lightly salted boiling water until soft. Drain, then transfer to a food processor or blender with 2 tablespoons heavy cream and a little salt and black pepper and process together until smooth. Stir in 1 tablespoon finely chopped cilantro leaves and serve. **Calories per serving 86**

spinach omelet arnold bennett

Calories per serving **349**
Serves **4**
Preparation time **15 minutes**
Cooking time **20–25 minutes**

1 (12 oz) package **fresh spinach**
1½ cups **milk**
8 oz **smoked haddock** or other **smoked fish**
1 teaspoon **black peppercorns**
3 tablespoons **unsalted butter**
1 tablespoon **rice flour**
5 **eggs**, lightly whisked
¼ cup grated **Parmesan cheese**
salt and **black pepper**

Put the spinach into a strainer and pour over boiling water until wilted. Set aside.

Put the milk, haddock, and peppercorns into a skillet and bring to a simmer, then cook for 5 minutes, until the fish is just cooked through. Lift out the fish, using a spatula, and let cool. Strain the milk into a small bowl.

Melt 2 tablespoons of the butter in a small saucepan, stir in the flour, and cook, stirring, for 1 minute. Add the strained milk, a little at a time, stirring continuously, until the sauce is creamy and thick. Simmer for 4–5 minutes.

Remove the skin and any bones from the fish, then flake the flesh into large pieces. Stir the wilted spinach and flaked fish into the sauce and season.

Melt the remaining butter in an ovenproof skillet, add the eggs, and cook for 3–4 minutes, until the eggs are still slightly liquid on top. Pour the sauce over the eggs, sprinkle with the cheese, and cook under a preheated hot broiler for 3–4 minutes, until golden and bubbling.

For eggs Florentine, put 2 egg yolks into a heatproof bowl over a saucepan of simmering water and beat for 4–5 minutes. Add 1½ teaspoons each of lemon juice and water and a pinch of salt and black pepper, then beat for another 1 minute. Add 7 tablespoons cubed butter, a few cubes at a time, beating continuously, until the sauce is the consistency of heavy cream. Poach 4 eggs (see page 88). Meanwhile, wilt 1 (12 oz) package fresh spinach as above. Divide the wilted spinach between 2 halved gluten-free whole-grain rolls, then top each one with a poached egg. Pour over the hollandaise sauce and serve. **Calories per serving 395**

lemon & sage sole

Calories per serving **319**
Serves **4**
Preparation time **10 minutes**
Cooking time **35–40 minutes**

1 lb **new potatoes**, scrubbed
a few **rosemary sprigs**
2 tablespoons **olive oil**
2 **soles** or **flounders**
    (about 8 oz each), filleted
    and pin-boned
grated zest and juice of
    1 **lemon**
¼ cup **heavy cream**
6 **sage leaves**, finely shredded
salt and **black pepper**

Cook the new potatoes in a saucepan of salted boiling water for 6–8 minutes, until almost tender. Drain and put into an ovenproof dish with the rosemary, drizzle with 1 tablespoon of the oil, and season with salt. Roast in a preheated oven, at 400°F, for 20 minutes, or until golden brown. Turn the oven off, but leave the potatoes in it to keep warm while you cook the fish.

Heat the remaining oil in a large skillet. Season the fish with salt and black pepper and place it, skin side down, in the hot pan. Cook for 3–4 minutes, or until the skin becomes crispy. Turn the fish over and cook for another 1 minute. Remove the fish from the pan and keep warm while you make the sauce.

Put the lemon zest and juice, cream, and sage into the pan and stir well to combine. Add a little water if the sauce becomes too thick.

Pour the sauce over the fish and serve with the roasted new potatoes.

For pan-fried sole with potato & fennel salad, put 1 lb cooked, warm new potatoes into a bowl with 1 finely shredded fennel bulb. Heat 1 tablespoon olive oil in a small skillet, add 1 tablespoon yellow mustard seeds, and cook until they begin to pop. Add these to the potatoes. Make the sauce as above, omitting the sage. Pour the sauce over the potatoes and fennel, season, and serve with the sole pan-fried as above.
Calories per serving 324

roasted pork loin with creamy veg

Calories per serving **387**
Serves **4**
Preparation time **10 minutes**
Cooking time **25–30 minutes**

1 teaspoon **ground cumin**
1 teaspoon **ground coriander**
1 lb **pork loin**, trimmed of fat
3 tablespoons **olive oil**
1 large **sweet potato** (about
    10 oz) peeled and chopped
2²/₃ cups shredded **savoy
    cabbage**
3 **leeks**, trimmed, cleaned,
    and sliced
3 tablespoons **sour cream**
2 teaspoons **no-added-sugar
    whole-grain mustard**

Mix together the spices in a bowl, then rub over the pork. Heat 1 tablespoon of the oil in an ovenproof skillet, add the pork, and cook until browned on all sides. Transfer to a preheated oven, at 350°F, and cook for 20–25 minutes, or until cooked through. Let rest for 2 minutes.

Meanwhile, cook the sweet potato in a saucepan of boiling water for 12–15 minutes, until tender, adding the cabbage and leeks 3–4 minutes before the end of the cooking time. Drain well.

Heat the remaining oil in a skillet, add the vegetables, and sauté for 7–8 minutes, until starting to turn golden. Stir in the cream and mustard.

Slice the pork and serve on top of the vegetables.

For broiled pork chops & mashed potatoes with cabbage & leek, cook 4 pork chops (about 5 oz each), trimmed of all fat, under a preheated hot broiler for 5 minutes on each side, or until cooked through. Meanwhile, cook 4 peeled and finely diced potatoes (about 1 lb), ½ head of finely shredded savoy cabbage, and 2 trimmed, cleaned, and finely sliced leeks in a saucepan of boiling water for 8 minutes, until tender. Drain, then mash in the pan with 2 tablespoons plain yogurt and salt and black pepper. Serve with the pork.
Calories per serving 324

cod saltimbocca

Calories per serving **322**
Serves **4**
Preparation time **10 minutes**
Cooking time **10 minutes**

4 skinless **cod loins**
  (about 5 oz each),
  halved lengthwise
8 slices of **prosciutto**
8 **sage leaves**
1 1/3 cups **frozen peas**
1 1/3 cups **frozen fava beans**
13 oz **asparagus**, trimmed
1 tablespoon **olive oil**

Wrap each cod loin in a slice of prosciutto, placing a sage leaf under the ends of each one.

Cook the peas, beans, and asparagus in a saucepan of simmering water for 4 minutes, until tender. Drain and remove the outer skins of the beans, if desired. Set aside.

Heat the oil in a skillet, add the fish, sage side down, and cook for 3 minutes, until the prosciutto is crisp, then turn over and cook for another 2 minutes, until the fish is cooked through. Remove the fish from the pan and keep warm.

Toss the vegetables in the oil in the pan, then transfer to 4 plates and top with the fish.

For prosciutto & figs, halve 8 figs lengthwise and cook them, cut side down, on a ridged grill pan for 1 minute, until charred. Sprinkle with 2 tablespoons balsamic vinegar while still warm, then wrap each one with 1/2 slice of prosciutto. Serve sprinkled with 2 tablespoons Parmesan cheese shavings and a few mint leaves. **Calories per serving 125**

wild rice jambalaya

Calories per serving **375**
  (not including bread)
Serves **4**
Preparation time **15 minutes**
Cooking time **35 minutes**

¾ cup **wild rice**
1 teaspoon **olive oil**
½ cup chopped **celery**
½ **red bell pepper**, cored,
  seeded, and diced
½ **green** or **yellow bell
  pepper**, cored, seeded,
  and diced
1 **onion**, chopped
1 **rindless lean bacon strip**,
  trimmed of fat
2 **garlic cloves**, crushed
2 tablespoons **tomato paste**
1 tablespoon chopped **thyme**
⅔ cup **long-grain rice**
1 **green chile,** seeded and
  finely chopped
½ teaspoon **cayenne pepper**
1⅔ cups drained canned
  tomatoes
1¼ cups **chicken broth**
⅔ cup **dry white wine**
8 oz medium **peeled shrimp**
chopped **parsley**, to garnish

Put the wild rice into a saucepan with water to cover.
Bring to a boil and boil for 5 minutes or according to the
package directions. Remove the pan from the heat and
cover tightly. Let steam for about 10 minutes, until the
grains are tender. Drain.

Heat the oil in a large nonstick skillet. Add the celery,
bell peppers, onion, bacon, and garlic. Cook, stirring, for
3–4 minutes, until the vegetables are soft. Stir in the
tomato paste and thyme. Cook for another 2 minutes.

Add the wild rice, long-grain rice, chile, cayenne pepper,
tomatoes, broth, and wine. Bring to a boil. Reduce the
heat and simmer for 10 minutes, until the rice is tender
but still firm to the bite.

Add the shrimp and cook, stirring occasionally, for
5 minutes, until the shrimp turn pink and are cooked
through. Spoon into 4 bowls. Sprinkle with parsley and
serve with crusty bread, if desired.

For chicken & shrimp jambalaya, omit the wild rice
and increase the quantity of long-grain rice to 1⅓ cups.
Soften the celery, bell peppers, onion, and garlic as
above, omitting the bacon. Remove from the pan and
heat 1 tablespoon of olive oil in the same pan. Add 4 oz
chicken breast, cut into chunks, and cook until golden
on all sides. Return the softened vegetables to the pan,
then add the remaining ingredients up to and including
the white wine. Bring to a boil, then complete the recipe
as above. **Calories per serving 396**

baked squash & goat cheese

Calories per serving **320**
Serves **4**
Preparation time **20 minutes**
Cooking time **25–30 minutes**

5 **raw beets** (about 13 oz),
 peeled and diced
1 ½ cups **butternut squash**,
 pumpkin, or other **winter**
 squash pieces (about
 1 ¼ lb before preparation)
1 **red onion**, cut into wedges
2 tablespoons **olive oil**
2 teaspoons **fennel seeds**
2 small **goat cheeses**
 (about 3 ½ oz each)
salt and **black pepper**
chopped **rosemary**, to garnish

Put the beets, squash, and onion into a roasting pan, drizzle with the oil, and sprinkle with the fennel seeds and salt and black pepper. Roast the vegetables in a preheated oven, at 400°F, for 20–25 minutes, turning once, until well browned and tender.

Cut the goat cheeses in to three and nestle each slice among the roasted vegetables. Sprinkle the cheeses with a little salt and black pepper and drizzle with some of the pan juices.

Return the dish to the oven for about 5 minutes, until the cheese is just beginning to melt. Sprinkle with rosemary and serve immediately.

For beet & pumpkin penne, roast the vegetables as above for 20–25 minutes, omitting the fennel seeds. Cook 11 ½ oz penne pasta in a saucepan of salted boiling water, then drain, reserving one ladleful of the cooking water. Return the pasta to the pan and add the roasted vegetables, a handful of torn basil leaves, and the cooking water. Omit the goat cheese and rosemary. Place over high heat, stirring, for 30 seconds and serve. **Calories per serving 485**

pork with pecans & apricots

Calories per serving **396**
Serves **4**
Preparation time **5 minutes**
Cooking time **10–15 minutes**

1 teaspoon **dried sage**
1 tablespoon **olive oil**
1¼ lb **pork tenderloin**
¾ cup **pecans**
8 **apricots**, halved and pitted
¼ cup **orange juice**
steamed **green beans**, to
   serve

Mix together the sage and oil, then rub the mixture over the pork before cutting it into thick medallions.

Heat a skillet, add the pork, and cook for 3–4 minutes on each side, until golden and cooked through. Remove from the pan and keep warm.

Add the pecans to the pan and cook for 2 minutes, until golden. Return the pork to the pan, add the apricots, and pour in the orange juice. Bring to a boil, then reduce the heat and simmer for 2–3 minutes.

Serve with steamed green beans.

For pork & apricot burgers, mix together 1 lb ground pork, 2 crushed garlic cloves, 1 teaspoon smoked paprika, 1 beaten egg, and 6 diced dried apricots in a bowl. Shape into 4 patties. Heat 1 tablespoon olive oil in a skillet and cook the patties for 6–7 minutes on each side, until cooked through. Serve with a crisp salad greens. **Calories per serving 328**

168

apricot & almond cake

Calories per serving **318**
Serves **6**
Preparation time **15 minutes,**
   plus cooling
Cooking time **50–55 minutes**

butter, for greasing
1 cup **dried apricots**
1 cup peeled, chopped
   sweet potato
½ cup **water**
3 **oranges**
3 **eggs**, separated
1 cup **ground almonds**
   (almond meal)
½ cup **rice flour**
1 teaspoon **baking powder**

To serve
1¼ cups **plain yogurt**
¼ teaspoon **ground**
   cinnamon

Grease an 8 inch cake pan with butter and line the bottom with nonstick parchment paper.

Put the apricots into a heatproof bowl, pour over enough boiling water to cover, and let soak for 1 minute. Drain, then chop three-quarters of the apricots, reserving the rest.

Put the chopped apricots, the sweet potato, and measured water into a saucepan and cook over low heat for 20–25 minutes, until the liquid is absorbed and the sweet potato and apricots are soft.

Put the cooked sweet potato and apricots, the reserved apricots, the grated zest and juice of 1 orange, and the egg yolks into a food processor or blender and blend until smooth. Whisk the egg whites in a clean bowl until stiff, then gently fold the apricot mixture into the whites. Fold in the almonds, flour, and baking powder.

Spoon the batter into the prepared pan, level the surface, and bake in a preheated oven, at 350°F, for 30 minutes, until a toothpick inserted into the center comes out clean. Let cool in the pan for 10 minutes.

Meanwhile, heat the juice and zest of the remaining oranges in a small saucepan and boil until reduced and syrupy.

Turn the cake out onto a serving plate and pour the syrup over it. Serve hot or cold, cut into 6 slices, with dollops of yogurt sprinkled with ground cinnamon.

maple apple cake

Calories per serving **312**
Serves **8**
Preparation time **10 minutes**
Cooking time **40–45 minutes**

½ cup plus **1** tablespoon
   coconut oil, melted, plus
   extra for greasing
1 ½ cups **whole-wheat flour**
1 teaspoon **baking powder**
½ teaspoon **ground
   cinnamon**
3–4 **Granny Smith** or other
   cooking apples (about
   1 ¼ lb), peeled, cored,
   and diced
⅓ cup **golden raisins**
⅓ cup **maple syrup**
2 **eggs**

Grease an 8 inch springform cake pan with coconut oil and line the bottom with nonstick parchment paper.

Put the flour, baking powder, and cinnamon into a bowl and mix well. Stir in the apples and golden raisins and mix to coat with the dry ingredients.

Whisk together the maple syrup, eggs, and coconut oil in a small bowl, then pour into the dry ingredients and mix together until well combined.

Spoon the batter into the prepared cake pan and level the top. Bake in a preheated oven, at 350°F, for 40–45 minutes, until a toothpick inserted in the center comes out clean. Transfer to a wire rack and let cool. Cut into 8 slices to serve.

For maple apple crisp, put 4 peeled, cored, and sliced sweet, crisp apples into an ovenproof baking dish. Put 2 cups oats, ⅓ cup coconut oil, ½ teaspoon ground cinnamon, and ¼ cup walnut pieces into a food processor and pulse briefly to break down the oats and walnuts. Sprinkle the mixture over the apples, then drizzle with ⅓ cup maple syrup. Bake in a preheated oven, at 400°F, for 15–18 minutes, until golden and crisp. Divide among 8 bowls and serve with crème fraîche or plain Greek yogurt, if desired. **Calories per serving 235 (not including crème fraîche)**

roasted rhubarb with coconut rice

Calories per serving **324**
Serves **4**
Preparation time **5 minutes**
Cooking time **15 minutes**

1½ tablespoons **honey**
8 **rhubarb stalks**, trimmed and chopped (about 3¼ cups prepared)
½ cup **basmati** or other **long-grain rice**
1⅔ cups **coconut milk**
½ cup **water**
1 tablespoon **toasted slivered almonds**

Heat 1 tablespoon of the honey in a small saucepan. Put the rhubarb into a roasting pan and pour the honey over it. Place in a preheated oven, at 400°F, for 10 minutes.

Meanwhile, put the rice, coconut milk, measured water, and remaining honey into a saucepan and bring to a simmer, then cook for 12–15 minutes, stirring occasionally, until the rice is tender.

Serve the rice pudding topped with the roasted rhubarb and sprinkled with a few slivered almonds.

banana & buttermilk pancakes

Calories per serving **315**
Serves **4**
Preparation time **10 minutes**
Cooking time **12–15 minutes**

1 cup **all-purpose flour**
1 teaspoon **baking powder**
pinch of **salt**
1 cup **buttermilk**
1 **egg**
2 small **bananas**, thinly sliced
1 tablespoon **vegetable oil**

To serve
1 **banana**, sliced
¼ cup chopped **pecans**
1 tablespoon **honey**

Sift the flour, baking powder, and salt into a large bowl and make a well in the center. Whisk together the buttermilk and egg in a small bowl, then gradually whisk into the flour mixture to form a smooth batter. Stir in the sliced bananas.

Heat a large nonstick skillet over medium heat. Dip a scrunched up piece of paper towel into the oil and use to wipe over the pan. Drop 3 large tablespoons of the batter into the pan to make 3 pancakes, spreading the batter out slightly with a spoon. Cook for 2–3 minutes, until bubbles start to appear on the surface and the underside is golden brown, then flip over and cook for another 2 minutes. Remove from the pan and keep warm. Repeat with the remaining batter to make 8 pancakes.

Serve the pancakes topped with extra sliced banana, sprinkled with pecans, and drizzled with a little honey.

For quick banana pancakes, warm 8 no-added-sugar prepared pancakes according to the package directions. Slice 4 bananas and divide among the pancakes. Fold them over and serve 2 pancakes per person drizzled with 1 teaspoon honey and 3 tablespoon fat-free plain Greek yogurt. **Calories per serving 326**

less than
500 calories

celery, apple & blue cheese salad

Calories per serving **488**
Serves **4**
Preparation time **10 minutes**
Cooking time **3–4 minutes**

½ cup **walnut halves**
2 cups crumbled **blue cheese**
3 tablespoons **white wine vinegar**
3 tablespoons **olive oil**
1 tablespoon **walnut oil**
½ teaspoon **honey**
4 **celery sticks**, thickly sliced diagonally
2 **green sweet, crisp apples**, cored and cut into wedges
16 sprigs of **watercress** or 1½ cups other **peppery greens**
1½ cups **arugula leaves**
black pepper

Heat a nonstick skillet over medium-low heat and dry-fry the walnuts for 3–4 minutes, stirring frequently, until golden and toasted. Set aside.

Put ⅔ cup of the blue cheese, the vinegar, oils, honey, and black pepper into a food processor or blender and process to a smooth creamy dressing, adding a little water if too thick.

Mix together the celery, apples, watercress, and arugula in a large bowl. Toss with the dressing and crumble the remaining cheese over the top.

Sprinkle over the toasted walnuts and serve.

For celery & blue cheese soup, melt 3 tablespoons butter in a saucepan, add 4 chopped celery sticks, and sauté for 5 minutes, until softened. Stir in 1 peeled and chopped potato, 1¼ cups milk, and 2½ cups vegetable broth and bring to a boil, then reduce the heat and simmer for 15–18 minutes, until the vegetables are tender. Using a handheld blender, blend until smooth. Sprinkle with 1⅔ cups crumbled blue cheese and season to taste. Ladle into 4 bowls and serve. **Calories per serving 394**

salmon, green lentil & dill salad

Calories per serving **460**
Serves **4**
Preparation time **30 minutes,
  plus cooling and chilling**
Cooking time **30–40 minutes**

1 lb **salmon fillet**
2 tablespoons **dry white wine**
4 **red bell peppers**
1 cup **green lentils**
large handful of **dill**, chopped
1 bunch of **scallions**, finely
  sliced
lemon juice
black pepper

Dressing
2 **green chiles**, seeded
  and chopped
large handful of **flat leaf
  parsley**, chopped
large handful of **dill**, chopped
2 **garlic cloves**
1 teaspoon **Dijon mustard**
½ cup **lemon juice**
1 tablespoon **olive oil**

Put the salmon on a sheet of aluminum foil and spoon the wine over it. Gather up the foil and fold over at the top to seal. Place on a baking sheet and bake in a preheated oven, at 400°F, for 15–20 minutes, until cooked through. Let cool, then flake, cover, and chill.

Broil the bell peppers and peel off the skins, following the directions on page 202. Reserve the juices.

Meanwhile, put the lentils in a large saucepan with plenty of water, bring to a boil, then simmer gently for 15–20 minutes, or according to package directions, until cooked but still firm to the bite.

Make the dressing. Process the chiles, parsley, dill, garlic, mustard, and lemon juice in a food processor until smooth. With the motor still running, drizzle in the oil through the feeder tube until the mixture is thick.

Drain the lentils, transfer to a bowl, and add the bell peppers and their juices. Add the dill, most of the scallions and season with black pepper. Stir in the dressing and let infuse.

Mix the flaked salmon through the lentils, adding a little lemon juice and the remaining scallions.

For salmon & potato salad, boil 13 oz new potatoes for 15–20 minutes, until tender. Drain and cool slightly, then lightly crush. Mix in ¼ cup olive oil, 2 tablespoons small capers, 1 bunch of sliced scallions, and salt and black pepper. Prepare the salmon as above and flake it through the potatoes. Add a handful of chopped dill and 1 bunch of watercress or 3½ cups of other peppery greens, then serve. **Calories per serving 383**

tomato & mozzarella salad

Calories per serving **429**
Serves **4**
Preparation time **10 minutes**
Cooking time **2 minutes**

2 tablespoons **pine nuts**
8 ripe **plum tomatoes**, sliced
6 **cherry tomatoes**, halved
1 small **red onion**, thinly sliced
small bunch of **basil**, leaves
   only
1½ cups **arugula leaves**
2 (8 oz) containers **mozzarella
   cheese balls**, torn
2 tablespoons **extra virgin
   olive oil**
2 tablespoons **balsamic
   vinegar**
salt and **black pepper**

Heat a nonstick skillet over medium-low heat and dry-fry the pine nuts, stirring frequently, until lightly golden and toasted. Set aside.

Put the tomatoes, onion, and basil into a serving bowl, season with salt and black pepper, and toss together.

Add the arugula and mozzarella and gently toss again.

Sprinkle with the pine nuts, drizzle with the olive oil and vinegar, and serve.

For tomato & basil soup, heat 1 tablespoon olive oil in a saucepan, add 1 diced red onion and 2 chopped garlic cloves, and sauté for 2–3 minutes, until softened. Add 3⅓ cups caned diced tomatoes, 2 tablespoons tomato paste, and 2 cups vegetable broth and bring to a boil, then reduce the heat and simmer for 30 minutes. Remove from the heat and stir in a handful of basil leaves and ½ teaspoon honey. Using a handheld blender, blend until smooth. Season to taste and stir through ½ cup chopped mozzarella cheese. Ladle into 4 bowls and serve. **Calories per serving 141**

curried egg salad

Calories per serving **473**
Serves **4**
Preparation time **10 minutes,
    plus cooling**
Cooking time **7–8 minutes**

8 **eggs**
4 **tomatoes**, cut into wedges
2 **Boston**, **Bibb**, or other small
    butterhead lettuce, leaves
    separated
¼ **cucumber**, sliced
1 cup **plain yogurt**
1 tablespoon **mild curry
    powder**
3 tablespoons **tomato paste**
juice of 2 **limes**
⅓ cup **no-added-sugar
    mayonnaise**
thyme leaves, to garnish
salt and **black pepper**

Bring a saucepan of water to a simmer, then gently lower the unshelled eggs into the water and cook for 7–8 minutes, until hard cooked. Drain and cool quickly under cold running water.

Shell the eggs, then halve and place on a large serving plate with the tomatoes, lettuce, and cucumber.

Mix together the yogurt, curry powder, tomato paste, lime juice, and mayonnaise. Season the dressing, then pour it over the salad. Serve immediately, garnished with thyme leaves.

For Indian-style spicy open omelet, heat 2 tablespoons vegetable oil in a large ovenproof skillet, add 1 chopped onion, 1 chopped red chile, 2 teaspoons cumin seeds, 1 teaspoon each of peeled and grated fresh ginger root and garlic, 1 teaspoon curry powder, and 1 finely chopped tomato. Stir-fry for 3–4 minutes. Beat together 6 eggs and a small handful of finely chopped cilantro. Season, then pour the eggs over the vegetable mixture and cook over low heat for 8–10 minutes, or until the bottom is starting to set. Put under a preheated hot broiler for 3–4 minutes, or until the top is set and lightly browned. Serve with warm naan or other flatbread and a salad, if desired. **Calories per serving 197 (not including naan and salad)**

broiled goat cheese salad

Calories per serving **453**
Serves **4**
Preparation time **15 minutes**
Cooking time **4–5 minutes**

⅓ cup **pine nuts**
2 teaspoons **orange blossom honey**
juice of 1 **lemon**
3 tablespoons **olive oil**
1 teaspoon **no-added-sugar whole-grain mustard**
1 **cucumber**, halved lengthwise, seeded, and thinly sliced
1¾ cups thinly sliced **radishes**
1 **red onion**, thinly sliced
2 tablespoons chopped **mint**
4 round **fromage de chèvre** or other **goat cheese** (about 3 oz each)

Heat a nonstick skillet over medium-low heat and dry-fry the pine nuts, stirring frequently, until lightly golden and toasted. Set aside.

Whisk together the honey, lemon juice, olive oil, and mustard in a small bowl. Set aside.

Put the cucumber into a large bowl and add the radish slices, onion, toasted pine nuts, and chopped mint and mix well.

Put the fromage de chèvre on a baking sheet and cook under a preheated hot broiler for 3–4 minutes, until golden and bubbling.

Pour the dressing over the salad and toss well. Divide among 4 plates and top each with a fromage de chèvre.

For goat cheese stuffed mushrooms, heat 1 tablespoon olive oil in a skillet, add 4 portobello mushrooms, and sauté for 3–4 minutes on each side. Divide 7 oz goat cheese evenly among the mushrooms and sprinkle with the leaves of 1 thyme sprig, 2 teaspoons honey, ¼ teaspoon freshly ground black pepper, 1 crushed garlic clove, and ½ cup chopped walnuts. Cook under a preheated broiler for 3–4 minutes, or until the cheese is melted and bubbling. **Calories per serving 295**

smoked trout & grape salad

Calories per serving **443**
Serves **2**
Preparation time **15 minutes**

7 oz **smoked trout**
1 cup **red seedless grapes**
¾ bunch or **watercress**
  or 3 cups other **peppery
  greens**
1 **fennel bulb**
3 tablespoons **no-added-
  sugar mayonnaise**
4 **small pickles**, finely diced
1½ tablespoons **capers**,
  chopped
2 tablespoons **lemon juice**
salt and **black pepper**

Flake the smoked trout into bite-size pieces, removing any bones, and put into a large salad bowl.

Wash and drain the grapes and watercress and add them to the bowl. Finely slice the fennel and add to the mix.

Mix together the mayonnaise, pickles, capers, and lemon juice in a small bowl. Season to taste with salt and black pepper, then carefully mix through the salad and serve.

For crispy trout salad, add 1 finely chopped hard-boiled egg, 2 finely chopped anchovy fillets, and 1 tablespoon chopped parsley to the dressing. Prepare the salad as above, adding 1 green sweet, crisp apple, cut into matchsticks. Season 2 pieces of fresh trout (about 5 oz each) with salt and black pepper. Heat 1 tablespoon vegetable oil in a skillet over high heat and cook the trout, skin side down, for 4 minutes, pressing it down with a spatula for an evenly crispy skin. Turn over the fish and cook for another 2 minutes, or until it is just cooked through. Remove from the pan. Toss the salad with the dressing and serve immediately with the crispy trout. **Calories per serving 432**

chicken & spinach chowder

Calories per serving **427**
Serves **6**
Preparation time **15 minutes**
Cooking time **35 minutes**

1 tablespoon **sunflower oil**
2 tablespoons **butter**
4 **smoked bacon strips,**
   chopped
2 small **leeks,** trimmed,
   cleaned, and thinly sliced,
   green and white parts
   separated
6 **Yukon gold** or **white round**
   potatoes (about 1½ lb),
   peeled and diced
3¾ cups **chicken broth**
1½ cups diced **cooked**
   chicken
2½ cups **low-fat milk**
⅔ cup **heavy cream**
2 cups coarsely chopped
   spinach
grated **nutmeg**
salt and **black pepper**

Heat the oil and butter in a large saucepan, add the bacon, white leeks, and diced potatoes, and cook over low heat for 5 minutes, stirring, until lightly golden.

Mix in the broth, then bring to a boil, cover, and simmer for 20 minutes, until the potatoes are just tender. Add the chicken and boil rapidly for 3 minutes.

Stir in the green leeks, milk, cream, and a little salt and black pepper. Simmer gently for 5 minutes, then stir in the spinach and a little nutmeg. Cook for 2 minutes, until the spinach is just cooked.

Ladle into 6 bowls, sprinkle with a little extra nutmeg, and serve.

For creamy chicken, bacon & celeriac soup, use
1 chopped onion in place of the leeks and replace the potatoes with celeriac. Cook with the bacon as above. Coarsely mash or puree the soup, then add the chicken and cook as above. Mix with cream and nutmeg but omit the spinach, adding 2 tablespoons chopped chives instead. **Calories per serving 353**

chicken parmigiana

Calories per serving **499**
Serves **4**
Preparation time **15 minutes,
plus chilling**
Cooking time **13–14 minutes**

4 **boneless, skinless chicken
breasts** (about 5 oz each)
2 **eggs**
1²/₃ cups **fresh whole-wheat
bread crumbs**
1 cup grated **Parmesan
cheese**
1 tablespoon **olive oil**
2 **garlic cloves**, crushed
2½ cups **tomato puree** or
tomato sauce
1 teaspoon **dried oregano**
1 cup shredded **mozzarella
cheese**
salad greens, to serve

Place the chicken breasts between 2 sheets of plastic wrap or wax paper and bang with a rolling pin or mallet until they are about ¼ inch thick.

Beat the eggs in a shallow bowl, then mix together the bread crumbs and half the grated Parmesan and put into a separate shallow bowl. Dip the chicken breasts first in the egg and then in the bread crumb and Parmesan mixture. Cover and chill for 15 minutes.

Cook the chicken under a preheated hot broiler for 5 minutes on each side, until cooked through.

Meanwhile, heat the oil in a pan, add the garlic, and sauté for 1 minute, then add the tomato puree and oregano and simmer for 5 minutes.

Pour the tomato sauce into an ovenproof dish and top with the chicken. Sprinkle with the mozzarella and remaining Parmesan and broil for 3–4 minutes, until the cheese has melted and the sauce is bubbling. Serve with crisp salad greens.

For chicken & Parmesan pasta, cook 10 oz gluten-free pasta in a saucepan of boiling water according to the package directions, adding 4 cups broccoli florets 3 minutes before the end of the cooking time. Meanwhile, heat 1 tablespoon olive oil in a skillet and cook 13 oz chopped chicken breasts for 8–10 minutes, until golden and cooked through, adding 2 crushed garlic cloves 2 minutes before the end of the cooking time. Drain the pasta and broccoli and add to the chicken, then stir in 2 tablespoons slivered almonds, 2 tablespoons chopped sun-dried tomatoes, and 2 tablespoons grated Parmesan. **Calories per serving 498**

cod with a cheese topping

Calories per serving **499**
Serves **4**
Preparation time **5 minutes**
Cooking time **15 minutes**

2 tablespoons **no-added-sugar whole-grain mustard**
3 tablespoons **beer** or **low-fat milk**
2 cups shredded **cheddar cheese**
2 tablespoons **olive oil**
4 pieces of **cod fillet** (about 7 oz each), pin-boned
salt and **black pepper**

Mix together the mustard, beer or milk, and cheese in a small saucepan, then put over low heat until the cheese melts. Stir occasionally and don't let it boil, because the cheese will curdle. Remove the pan from the heat and let cool and thicken.

Heat a skillet over high heat with the oil. Season the fish, place it in the pan, skin side down, and cook for 4–5 minutes, until the skin is crispy, then turn the fish over and cook for another 1 minute, until cooked through.

Spread the cheese mixture over the 4 pieces of cod and put under a preheated broiler and cook until golden brown.

For whole-grain mustard & cream sauce, to serve as an accompaniment, in a small saucepan sweat 2 finely chopped shallots and 1 crushed garlic clove in 1 tablespoon olive oil. Add ½ cup chicken broth and 1 cup heavy cream to the pan and bring to a boil. Stir in 1 tablespoon no-added-sugar whole-grain mustard. **Calories per serving 262**

peppered beef with potato cakes

Calories per serving **455**
Serves **4**
Preparation time **15 minutes**
Cooking time **15–20 minutes**

½ cup **balsamic vinegar**
2 tablespoons **cracked black peppercorns**
2 lean **sirloin steaks** (about 7 oz each)
2–3 **sweet potatoes** (about 1 lb 2 oz), peeled and shredded
2 **eggs**, beaten
2 tablespoons **chickpea flour**
½ cup grated **Parmesan cheese**
2 tablespoons **peanut oil**
3½ cups **arugula leaves**
salt and **black pepper**

Pour the balsamic into a small saucepan and simmer until reduced by half and it forms a syrupy glaze. Set aside.

Put the cracked peppercorns onto a board or plate and press each steak into it. Heat a ridged grill pan and cook the steaks for 3–4 minutes on each side, depending on how rare you prefer your steak. Let rest for 5 minutes, then slice into thick slices.

Meanwhile, mix together the sweet potatoes, eggs, chickpea flour, Parmesan, and salt and black pepper in a bowl. Heat the oil in a large skillet, add spoonfuls of the batter to the pan, and flatten with a spatula. Cook for 2–3 minutes on each side, until crisp and golden. Remove from the pan and keep warm. Repeat with the remaining mixture.

Arrange 2 sweet potato cakes on each plate, then top with the arugula and slices of steak. Serve drizzled with the balsamic glaze.

For stuffed sweet potatoes, bake 4 sweet potatoes in a preheated oven, at 400°F, for 1 hour until soft. When cool enough to handle, cut in half lengthwise and scoop out the flesh into a bowl. Reserve the skins. Add 4 chopped scallions, 1 cup grated Manchego or Parmesan cheese, and 2 tablespoons sour cream to the bowl and mix together, then spoon back into the potato skins. Cook 6 pancetta strips under a preheated hot broiler until crisp. Sprinkle on top of the potatoes to serve. **Calories per serving 320**

potato pizza margherita

Calories per serving **478**
Serves **4**
Preparation time **20 minutes,
plus cooling**
Cooking time **45 minutes**

8 **russet potatoes** (about
  2 lb), peeled and cut into
  small chunks
3 tablespoons **olive oil**,
  plus extra for oiling
1 **egg**, beaten
2/3 cup grated **Parmesan
  cheese** or 1 cup shredded
  cheddar cheese
1/4 cup **no-added-sugar
  ketchup**
5 small **tomatoes** (about 1 lb),
  thinly sliced
4 oz **mozzarella cheese**,
  thinly sliced
1 tablespoon chopped **thyme**,
  plus extra sprigs to garnish
  (optional)
salt

Cook the potatoes in a saucepan of salted boiling water for 15 minutes, or until tender. Drain well, return to the pan, and let cool for 10 minutes.

Add 2 tablespoons of the oil, the egg, and half the grated cheese to the potato and mix well. Turn out onto an oiled baking sheet and spread out to form a 10 inch circle. Place in a preheated oven, at 400°F, for 15 minutes.

Remove from the oven and spread with the ketchup. Arrange the tomatoes and mozzarella slices on top. Sprinkle with the remaining grated cheese, thyme, if using, and a little salt. Drizzle with the remaining oil.

Return to the oven for another 15 minutes, until the potato is crisp around the edges and the cheese is melting. Cut into 4 wedges, garnish with thyme sprigs, if desired, and serve.

For salami potato pizza, make as above, adding 4 slices of chopped salami with the tomato and mozzarella to the top of the pizza. Continue as above. Calories per serving 499

moroccan chicken & harissa

Calories per serving **433**
  (not including rice)
Serves **4**
Preparation time **20 minutes,
  plus cooling**
Cooking time **40 minutes**

1 **onion**, finely chopped
2 teaspoons **paprika**
1 teaspoon **cumin seeds**
4 **boneless, skinless chicken
  breasts** (about 4 oz each)
bunch of **cilantro**, finely
  chopped
¼ cup **lemon juice**
3 tablespoons **olive oil**
salt and **black pepper**

Harissa
4 **red bell peppers**
4 large **red chiles**
2 **garlic cloves**, crushed
½ teaspoon **coriander seeds**
1 teaspoon **caraway seeds**
⅓ cup **olive oil**

Make the harissa. Heat a ridged grill pan or skillet, add the whole red bell peppers, and cook for 15 minutes, turning occasionally. The skins will blacken and start to lift. Place the bell peppers in a plastic bag, seal the bag, and set aside for a while (this encourages them to "sweat," making it easier to remove their skins). When cool enough to handle, remove the skin, cores, and seeds from the bell peppers and put the flesh into a blender or food processor.

Remove the skin, cores, and seeds from the red chiles in the same way and add the chile flesh to the blender, together with the garlic, coriander and caraway seeds, and olive oil. Process in the blender to a smooth paste. If not required immediately, put the harissa into a sealable container and pour a thin layer of olive oil over the top. Cover with a lid and refrigerate.

Put the onion into a bowl, add the paprika and cumin seeds, and mix together. Rub the onion and spice mixture into the chicken breasts. Heat the cleaned pan, add the chicken, and cook for 10 minutes on each side, turning once, until cooked through.

Put the cilantro into a bowl and add the lemon juice, olive oil, and a little seasoning. Add the chicken to the bowl and toss well. Serve with the harissa and brown rice, if desired.

For a spinach salad, to serve as an accompaniment, rinse and tear 1⅓ (10 oz) packages fresh spinach and add to a saucepan with any residual water. Cover and cook for 1–2 minutes, until wilted. Stir in 1 chopped garlic clove, ½ cup Greek yogurt, season, and warm through. **Calories per serving 55**

spicy baby broccoli pasta

Calories per serving **405**
Serves **4**
Preparation time **5 minutes**
Cooking time **10–12 minutes**

11½ oz **spaghetti**
7 oz **baby broccoli**
2 tablespoons **olive oil**
8 **scallions**, chopped
½ teaspoon **dried red pepper flakes**
juice of ½ **lemon**
salt and **black pepper**
¼ cup grated **Parmesan cheese**, to serve

Cook the spaghetti in a saucepan of boiling water according to the package directions.

Meanwhile, blanch the baby broccoli in a separate saucepan of boiling water for 2 minutes, then drain and refresh under cold running water.

Heat the oil in a skillet, add the baby broccoli and scallions, and cook over medium heat for 4–5 minutes, until softened.

Drain the pasta, then stir into the vegetables with the dried red pepper flakes and lemon juice. Season well and serve sprinkled with the grated Parmesan.

For broccoli & pasta salad, cook 11½ oz pasta shapes in a saucepan of boiling water according to the package directions, adding 7 oz trimmed baby broccoli 2 minutes before the end of the cooking time. Drain and refresh under cold running water, then toss together with ⅔ cup crumbled feta cheese, 4 sliced scallions, 10 halved pitted olives, 2 tablespoons olive oil, and 1 tablespoon balsamic vinegar. Serve sprinkled with 2 tablespoons toasted pecans. **Calories per serving 495**

lime & cilantro sea bass

Calories per serving **486**
Serves **4**
Preparation time **20 minutes,
    plus chilling**
Cooking time **10 minutes**

1 ¼ sticks butter, softened
3 tablespoons chopped
    cilantro, plus small bunch
1 large **red chile,** seeded and
    finely chopped
2 **limes**
4 whole **sea bass** (about
    10 oz each), cleaned
2 tablespoons **vegetable oil**
salt and **black pepper**

Mix together the butter, chopped cilantro, chile, and grated zest of the limes in a bowl. Season with salt and black pepper. Take a sheet of plastic wrap and spoon on the butter mixture. Roll the plastic wrap up to form a cylinder, then twist the ends to enclose the butter and put into the refrigerator to set.

Make 3 slits in the flesh on each side of the fish, making sure you don't cut all the way through it. Slice the grated limes and place a few slices of lime in the cavity of each fish, along with some cilantro sprigs.

Brush the outside of the fish lightly with the oil and season both sides generously with salt and black pepper. Place the fish directly on the rack of a medium-hot barbecue or first in a fish grill (this is easier). Cook the fish for 5 minutes on each side. The best way to test if the fish is cooked is by looking inside the cavity to see if the flesh has become opaque or if the fish is firm to the touch.

Slice the butter thinly into disks and place a slice in each of the cuts you made on 1 side of the fish. Let the butter melt. Serve with a green salad.

For barbecued sea bass packages, butter 4 large square pieces of aluminum foil and place a sea bass in the center of each piece. Drizzle with 2 tablespoons olive oil and place a few pieces of chopped chile and ginger and a couple of slices of lime in each package. Seal the foil to form packages and place on a medium-hot barbecue grill rack or under a medium-hot broiler for 8–10 minutes, or until the fish turns opaque. **Calories per serving 206**

corned beef hash

Calories per serving **481**
Serves **4**
Preparation time **10 minutes**
Cooking time **20–25 minutes**

5 **russet potatoes**, peeled
   (about 1¼ lb)
3 tablespoons **olive oil**
1 **onion**, chopped
11½ oz canned **corned beef**
2 **tomatoes**, chopped
4 **eggs**

Cook the potatoes in a saucepan of boiling water for 12–14 minutes, until tender.

Meanwhile, heat 1 tablespoon of oil in a large skillet, add the onion, and sauté for 4–5 minutes, until softened. Add the corned beef to the pan and cook for another 2–3 minutes.

Drain the potatoes and add them to the pan, cooking and lightly crushing them for 1–2 minutes. Stir in the tomatoes and cook for another 3–4 minutes.

Meanwhile, heat the remaining oil in another skillet and cook the eggs to your preference.

Serve the corned beef hash topped with a fried egg.

For corned beef, egg & salad baguettes, slice 2 gluten-free baguettes in half horizontally and toast each piece for 2–3 minutes on each side. Spread the bottom half of each baguette with a teaspoon of butter, then top with ¼ shredded iceberg lettuce, 1 sliced hard-boiled egg, and 3 oz of canned corned beef, sliced. Sandwich together with the remaining baguettes and cut each baguette in half. **Calories per half baguette 487**

salmon with fava bean salad

Calories per serving **461**
Serves **4**
Preparation time **15 minutes**
Cooking time **10–15 minutes**

4⅓ cups shelled **fresh** or
  frozen fava beans
2 tablespoons chopped **mint**
1 tablespoon chopped **dill**
3 tablespoons **lemon juice**
3 tablespoons **olive oil**
2 teaspoons **Dijon mustard**
4 **salmon fillets** (about 5 oz
  each), skin on
1 teaspoon **sea salt**
1 teaspoon **cracked black**
  peppercorns
lemon wedges, to serve

Cook the fava beans in a saucepan of boiling water for 5–6 minutes, or until tender, then drain and remove the skins. Put the beans into a bowl and toss with the mint, dill, lemon juice, 2 tablespoons of the oil, and the mustard.

Sprinkle the skin of the salmon with the salt and black peppercorns. Heat the remaining oil in a large skillet, add the salmon, skin side down, and cook for 4–5 minutes, until the skin is golden and crisp. Turn the fish over and cook for another 2–3 minutes, or until the salmon is cooked through and to your preference.

Divide the fava bean salad among 4 plates, top with the salmon, and serve with lemon wedges.

For salmon & fava bean fish cakes, cook 3 peeled and chopped russet potatoes in a saucepan of boiling water for 15–18 minutes, until tender, adding 1½ cups fava beans 5 minutes before the end of the cooking time. Drain and mash together. Meanwhile, cook 10 oz skinless salmon fillet under a preheated hot broiler for 4–5 minutes on each side, or until cooked through, then flake into big pieces and stir into the mash with 1 tablespoon chopped dill and salt and black pepper. Shape into 4 fish cakes and dust with 1 tablespoon chickpea flour. Heat 2 tablespoons olive oil in a skillet and cook the fish cakes for 3–4 minutes on each side, until heated through. Serve with a crisp green salad.
Calories per serving 377

roasted summer vegetables

Calories per serving **418**
Serves **4**
Preparation time **15 minutes**
Cooking time **45–50 minutes**

1 **red bell pepper**, cored,
  seeded, and thickly sliced
1 **yellow bell pepper**, cored,
  seeded, and thickly sliced
1 **eggplant**, cut into chunks
2 **yellow** or **green zucchini**,
  cut into chunks
1 **red onion**, cut into wedges
6 **garlic cloves**
2 tablespoons **extra virgin
  canola** or **olive oil**
4–5 **thyme sprigs**
8–12 **yellow** and **red baby
  plum tomatoes** (about 5 oz)
1 cup **hazelnuts**
4 cups **arugula leaves**
2 tablespoons **raspberry** or
  balsamic vinegar
salt and **black pepper**
handful of **mustard cress** or
  other **peppery microgreens**,
  to garnish (optional)

Toss all the vegetables, except the tomatoes, in a large bowl with the oil. Season with a little salt and black pepper and add the thyme. Transfer to a large roasting pan and put into a preheated oven, at 375°F, for 40–45 minutes, or until the vegetables are tender. Add the tomatoes and return to the oven for another 5 minutes, or until the tomatoes are just softened and beginning to burst.

Meanwhile, put the hazelnuts into a small roasting pan and place in the oven for 10–12 minutes, or until golden and the skin is peeling away. Let cool, then remove the excess skin and crush lightly.

Toss the arugula leaves gently with the roasted vegetables and pile onto 4 large plates. Sprinkle with the crushed hazelnuts and drizzle with the vinegar. Sprinkle with the mustard cress, if desired, and serve immediately.

For roasted vegetable pasta, roast the vegetables as above, then put into a large saucepan with 2 cups tomato puree or sauce and ⅔ cup vegetable broth. Bring to a boil, then reduce the heat and simmer gently for 20 minutes. Remove from the heat and, using a handheld blender, blend until smooth. Season with salt and black pepper to taste and serve with 1 ½ lb hot cooked pasta. **Calories per serving 461**

lamb with mashed potatoes & peas

Calories per serving **491**
Serves **4**
Preparation time **10 minutes**
Cooking time **12–15 minutes**

6–7 **russet potatoes** (about
  1 lb 10 oz), peeled and
  chopped
2⅓ cups **frozen** or **fresh peas**
1 tablespoon chopped
  rosemary
8 **lamb cutlets** (about
  3½ oz each)
2 tablespoons **butter**
salt and **black pepper**

Cook the potatoes in a saucepan of boiling water for
12–15 minutes, until tender, adding the peas 2 minutes
before the end of the cooking time.

Meanwhile, sprinkle half the rosemary over the lamb
cutlets, then cook them under a preheated hot broiler
for 3–4 minutes on each side, depending on how pink
you prefer your lamb. Let rest.

Drain the potatoes and peas, then return to the pan
and lightly mash with the remaining rosemary, butter,
and salt and black pepper to taste. Serve the lamb
cutlets with the mashed potatoes and peas.

For rosemary lamb cutlets with summer salad,

mix together 2 tablespoons chopped rosemary and
1 tablespoon olive oil in a small bowl, then rub over
8 lamb cutlets. Cook under a preheated hot broiler for
3–4 minutes on each side, depending on how pink
you prefer your lamb. Meanwhile, cook ⅔ cup fresh or
frozen peas, ½ cup fava beans, and 4 oz asparagus
tips in a saucepan of boiling water for 2–3 minutes.
Drain, refresh under cold running water, and drain again,
then toss together with 2 carrots, peeled and cut into
matchsticks, 12 baby corn, the torn leaves of 1 romaine
lettuce, a small handful of mint leaves, and 12 cherry
tomatoes in a serving bowl. Drizzle with 2 tablespoons
extra virgin olive oil and the juice of 1 lemon. Serve with
the lamb. **Calories per serving 376**

turkey croque madame

Calories per serving **499**
Serves **4**
Preparation time **10 minutes**
Cooking time **8–10 minutes**

8 thick **whole-grain bread slices** (about 1½ oz each), from a large, round loaf
3 tablespoons **no-added-sugar whole-grain mustard**
1¾ cups shredded **reduced-fat sharp cheddar cheese**
7 oz **cooked turkey**, thinly sliced
2 **tomatoes**, sliced
2 **scallions**, thinly sliced
1 tablespoon **distilled white vinegar**
4 **extra-large eggs**
3½ cups **baby leaf spinach**
black pepper
chopped **chives**, to garnish

Lay 4 slices of the bread on a board and spread each slice with the mustard. Divide half of the cheese among them, then all of the turkey and tomato slices. Sprinkle with the scallions, season with black pepper, and sprinkle with the remaining cheddar. Top with the remaining slices of bread.

Heat a large, nonstick skillet over medium heat until hot, then carefully add the sandwiches and cook for 4–5 minutes, or until golden and crispy. Turn the sandwiches over and cook for another 4–5 minutes. Alternatively, toast in a flat-surfaced panini machine according to the manufacturer's directions.

Meanwhile, bring a large saucepan of water to a gentle simmer, add the vinegar, and stir with a large spoon to create a swirl. Carefully break 2 eggs into the water and cook for 3 minutes. Remove with a slotted spoon and keep warm. Repeat with the remaining eggs.

Transfer each sandwich to a serving plate, sprinkle with a few spinach leaves, and top with a poached egg. Garnish with chives and serve immediately.

For turkey & cheese sandwiches, cut 1 whole-grain baguette almost in half lengthwise. Cut into 4 and place, opened out, on a baking sheet. Top as above with the mustard, turkey, tomatoes, and scallions. Sprinkle with all of the shredded cheese. Cook under a preheated hot broiler for 3–4 minutes or until hot and melted. Serve hot with baby leaf spinach, if desired. **Calories per serving 437**

hake on creamed spinach

Calories per serving **499**
Serves **4**
Preparation time **4 minutes**
Cooking time **15 minutes**

4 pieces of **hake** (about
  7 oz each)
2 tablespoons **olive oil**
2 **shallots**, finely chopped
1 **garlic clove**, crushed
2 cups **white wine**
1 lb **baby spinach leaves**
½ cup **heavy cream**
½ cup **pine nuts**
salt and **black pepper**

Place the hake in an ovenproof dish, drizzle with 1 tablespoon of the oil, and season with salt and black pepper. Place Put into a preheated oven, at 400°F, for 6–8 minutes, or until the fish is firm.

Meanwhile, heat the remaining oil in a large skillet, add the shallots, and sauté gently until softened. Add the garlic and sauté for another 1 minute. Pour in the wine and let simmer until all the liquid has evaporated.

Add the spinach to the pan, in batches, letting it wilt completely, then stir in the cream and season with salt and black pepper.

Heat a nonstick skillet over medium-low heat and dry-fry the pine nuts, stirring frequently, until lightly golden and toasted.

Place some creamed spinach in the center of each plate, top with a piece of fish, and sprinkle some toasted pine nuts over the top.

beet risotto

Calories per serving **498**
Serves **4**
Preparation time **15 minutes**
Cooking time **1 hour**

6 **raw beets** (about 1 lb),
 peeled and diced
2 tablespoons **olive oil**
2 tablespoons **water**
pinch of **dried sage**
1 large **onion**, diced
2 **garlic cloves**, crushed
1½ cups **risotto rice**
4¼ cups hot **vegetable broth**
3½ oz **goat cheese**
salt and **black pepper**

To serve
¼ cup grated **Parmesan
 cheese**
2–3 chopped **sage leaves**

Toss the beets in half the oil and season well. Wrap in aluminum foil and cook in a preheated oven, at 400°F, for 30–35 minutes, until tender.

Put half of the beets into a food processor or blender with the measured water and dried sage and blend to a puree. Set aside.

Heat the remaining oil in a saucepan, add the onion, and sauté for 3–4 minutes, until softened. Add the garlic and rice and stir well. Add a ladle of the broth and cook, stirring, until all the liquid has been absorbed. Continue to add the remaining broth in the same way until the rice is almost tender.

Stir in the cooked diced beets and the beet puree and continue to cook, stirring, for 8–10 minutes, until the rice is cooked through. Stir in the goat cheese and serve sprinkled with the Parmesan cheese and chopped sage.

For roasted beet & goat cheese salad, put 3–4 raw beets (about 10 oz), peeled and cut into wedges, into a roasting pan and toss with 1 tablespoon olive oil and 1 teaspoon cumin seeds. Roast as above for 35–40 minutes. Meanwhile, whisk together 2 tablespoons olive oil, 1 tablespoon balsamic vinegar, ½ teaspoon no-added-sugar whole-grain mustard, and ½ teaspoon maple syrup in a small bowl. Separate 2 oranges into sections and toss with ½ bunch of watercress or 2 cups of other peppery greens, 1 peeled, pitted, and sliced avocado, 2 tablespoons pumpkin seeds, and ¼ sliced cucumber in a serving bowl. Broil 4 (2¼ oz) goat cheeses until golden. Add the roasted beets to the salad and toss with the dressing. Top with the goat cheese and serve. **Calories per serving 468**

indian fish curry

Calories per serving **446**
 (not including rice)
Serves **4**
Preparation time **15 minutes**
Cooking time **30 minutes**

2 tablespoons **vegetable oil**
1 **onion**, finely chopped
1 **red chile,** seeded and
 finely chopped
1 **garlic clove**, crushed
2 inch piece of **fresh ginger
 root**, peeled and finely
 chopped
1 tablespoon **ground cumin**
1 tablespoon **ground
 coriander**
1 teaspoon **turmeric**
1 teaspoon **garam masala**
1²/₃ cups canned **diced
 tomatoes**
1²/₃ cups **coconut milk**
2 large **monkfish tails**, cut
 into chunks
12 **peeled jumbo shrimp**
8 oz **fresh mussels**, scrubbed
 and debearded (discard any
 that don't shut when tapped)
small bunch of **cilantro** or
 parsley, coarsely chopped

Heat the oil in a large skillet, add the onion, and sauté gently for about 10 minutes, until golden brown. Add the chile, garlic, ginger, and dried spices and cook for another 1 minute, until fragrant.

Add the tomatoes and coconut milk and bring to a boil, then reduce the heat and simmer for about 10 minutes, until the curry sauce has thickened.

Stir in the monkfish and shrimp and cook for 3–4 minutes, until the fish is just cooked through and the shrimp turn pink. Add the mussels and cook for another 3–4 minutes or until they have opened. Discard any that remain closed.

Season and stir through the chopped herbs. Serve with basmati rice, if desired.

For garlic & black mustard seed naans, to serve as an accompaniment, heat 1 tablespoon oil in a small skillet, add 1 tablespoon black mustard seeds, and cook until they start to pop. Mix together 7 tablespoons softened butter with the mustard seeds and 1 crushed garlic clove and spread this mixture over 2 large naans (available at Indian grocery stores). Place the 2 buttered sides together and wrap in aluminum foil. Bake in a preheated oven, at 350°F, for 10 minutes, until warmed through. Cut into 4 and serve. **Calories per serving 380**

spicy lamb meatball pitas

Calories per serving **431**
Serves **4**
Preparation time **20 minutes**
Cooking time **10–12 minutes**

1 ½ teaspoons **peanut oil**
4 **whole-grain pita breads**
lemon wedges, to serve

Lamb meatballs
1 small **onion**, chopped
2 **garlic cloves**, crushed
13 oz **lean ground lamb**
1 cup **fresh whole-grain bread crumbs**
1 medium **egg**, lightly beaten
1 small bunch of **parsley**, chopped
1 small bunch of **cilantro**, chopped
½–¾ teaspoon **ground cinnamon**
1 tablespoon **ground paprika**
1 ½ teaspoons **ground cumin**
salt and **black pepper**

Salad
1 **carrot**, peeled and grated
6 **radishes**, thinly sliced
½ **iceberg lettuce**, shredded
½ **cucumber**, thinly sliced

Put all the meatball ingredients into a food processor and pulse several times until well combined. Put into a large bowl and, using wet hands, shape the mixture into 16 meatballs.

Heat the peanut oil in a large, nonstick skillet over medium heat, add the meatballs, and cook for 10–12 minutes, turning frequently, until cooked through and browned all over. Remove with a slotted spoon and drain on paper towels.

Meanwhile, wrap the pita breads in aluminum foil and put into a preheated oven, at 350°F, for 5–8 minutes, or until warm. To make the salad, mix the carrot, radishes, lettuce, and cucumber in a bowl.

Slice open the warm pitas, fill with the salad, and then add the meatballs. Serve immediately with lemon wedges to squeeze over the filling.

For barbecued lamb skewers, make the lamb mixture as above. Put into a large bowl and form into flat cylinder shapes around 4 long, flat metal skewers. Cook on a barbecue grill rack or under a preheated hot broiler for 10–12 minutes, or until cooked through, then serve with the pita breads and salad as above. **Calories per serving 431**

mediterranean cauliflower pizzas

Calories per serving **443**
Serves **4**
Preparation time **20 minutes**
Cooking time **1 hour**

2 heads of **cauliflower**,
  coarsely chopped
2 **eggs**
½ cup shredded **cheddar**
  cheese
½ cup grated **Parmesan**
  cheese
1 teaspoon **cayenne pepper**
large pinch of **sea salt**
¼ cup **tomato paste**
1 **red bell pepper**, cored,
  seeded, and sliced
1 **zucchini**, thinly sliced
1 **garlic clove**, finely sliced
4 **artichoke hearts**, quartered
1 teaspoon **dried oregano**
8 oz **mozzarella cheese**,
  sliced

Line a baking sheet with nonstick parchment paper.

Put the cauliflower into a food processor or blender and process until fine. Transfer to a dry skillet and cook for 10 minutes, stirring occasionally, to get rid of the moisture.

Transfer the cauliflower to a large bowl and stir in the eggs, cheeses, cayenne pepper, and salt. Divide the mixture in half and spoon onto the prepared baking sheet in 2 mounds, using your hands to shape into rough circles.

Put into a preheated oven, at 350°F, for 30 minutes, until they hold their shape and are golden. Using a spatula, flip each one over and bake for another 10 minutes.

Remove from the oven and spread with the tomato paste, then top with the vegetables, oregano, and mozzarella. Return to the oven and bake for 10 minutes. Cut each pizza in half, then serve immediately.

For cauliflower cheese soup, heat 1 tablespoon olive oil in a saucepan, add 1 chopped onion, and sauté for 4–5 minutes, until softened. Add 1 large head of cauliflower, trimmed and chopped, 1 peeled and chopped Yukon gold or white round potato, and 5 cups vegetable broth and bring to a boil. Simmer for 20–25 minutes, until the vegetables are soft, then stir in 1 cup crumbled feta cheese. Using a handheld blender, blend until smooth. Season to taste, then serve with a sprinkling of grated Parmesan. **Calories per serving 311**

cheesy pork with parsnip puree

Calories per serving **480**
 (not including green beans)
Serves **4**
Preparation time **10 minutes**
Cooking time **16–20 minutes**

4 lean **pork cutlets** (about
 4 oz each)
1 teaspoon **olive oil**
½ cup crumbled or shredded
 Wensleydale or **cheddar
 cheese**
1½ teaspoons chopped **sage**
1⅔ cups **fresh whole-grain
 bread crumbs**
1 **egg yolk**, beaten
black pepper

Parsnip puree

6 **parsnips** (about 1¼ lb),
 chopped
2 **garlic cloves**
3 tablespoons **crème fraîche**
 or **plain Greek yogurt**

Season the pork with plenty of black pepper. Heat
the oil in a nonstick skillet, add the pork, and cook for
2 minutes on each side, until browned, then transfer to
an ovenproof dish.

Mix together the cheese, sage, bread crumbs, and
egg yolk. Divide the mixture into 4 and use to top each
of the pork cutlets, pressing down gently. Cook in a
preheated oven, at 400°F, for 12–15 minutes, until
the topping is golden.

Meanwhile, make the puree. Put the parsnips and
garlic into a saucepan of boiling water and cook for
10–12 minutes, until tender.

Drain and mash with the crème fraîche and plenty of
black pepper. Serve with the pork cutlets and steamed
green beans, if desired.

For chicken with breaded tomato topping, replace
the pork with 4 boneless, skinless chicken breasts
(about 5 oz each). Brown and lay in an ovenproof
dish, as above. Make the topping as above, replacing
the sage with 4 chopped sun-dried tomatoes and
¼ teaspoon dried oregano. Bake as above and serve
with the parsnip puree. **Calories per serving 475**

nutty passion fruit yogurts

Calories per serving **428**
Serves **2**
Preparation time **5 minutes,
  plus chilling**

2 **passion fruit**
1 cup **plain yogurt**
¼ cup **honey**
½ cup **roasted hazelnuts,**
  coarsely chopped
4 **clementines**, peeled and
  chopped into small pieces

Halve the passion fruit and scoop the pulp into a large bowl. Add the yogurt and mix them together gently.

Put 2 tablespoons of the honey into the bottom of 2 narrow glasses and sprinkle with half of the hazelnuts. Spoon half of the yogurt over the nuts and arrange half of the clementine pieces on top of the yogurt.

Repeat the layering, reserving a few of the nuts for decoration. Sprinkle the nuts over the top and chill the yogurts until ready to serve.

For passion fruit, coconut & strawberry yogurts, soak 2 tablespoons dry unsweetened coconut in ¼ cup skim milk for 30 minutes. Mix the passion fruit and yogurt as above, also folding in the soaked coconut. Layer as above, omitting the hazelnuts and replacing the clementines with ⅔ cup quartered, hulled strawberries. **Calories per serving 199**

rosemary panna cottas

Calories per serving **456**
Serves **6**
Preparation time **15 minutes,**
   plus soaking, cooling, and
   chilling
Cooking time **15 minutes**

3 tablespoons **cold water**
1 envelope or **1** tablespoon
   powdered gelatin
2 cups **heavy cream**
²/₃ cup **milk**
¼ cup **thick honey**
2 teaspoons finely chopped
   rosemary leaves
small **rosemary sprigs,**
   to decorate

Apricot compote
1 ¼ cups d**ried apricots,**
   sliced
1 ¼ cups **water**
1 tablespoon **thick honey**
2 teaspoons finely chopped
   rosemary leaves

Spoon the measured water into a small heatproof bowl or mug. Sprinkle the gelatin over it and tilt the bowl or mug so that all the dry powder is absorbed by the water. Let soak for 5 minutes.

Pour the cream and milk into a saucepan, add the honey, and bring to a boil. Add the soaked gelatin, remove the pan from the heat, and stir until completely dissolved. Add the rosemary and let stand for 20 minutes for the flavors to infuse, stirring from time to time. Pour the cream mixture into 6 individual ²/₃ cup metal molds, straining, if preferred. Let cool completely, then chill for 4–5 hours, until set.

Put all the compote ingredients into a saucepan, cover, and simmer for 10 minutes, then let cool.

Dip the molds into hot water for 10 seconds, loosen the edges, then turn out the panna cottas onto small serving plates and spoon the compôte around them. Decorate the panna cottas with the rosemary sprigs.

For vanilla panna cottas, make the panna cotta as above but without the rosemary, adding the seeds from 1 slit vanilla bean and the bean itself as the cream mixture cools. Discard the bean just before pouring the mixture into the molds, then continue as above. Turn out and serve with fresh raspberries, if desired. **Calories per serving 456 (not including raspberries)**

raw raspberry & nut tarts

Calories per serving **418**
Makes **6**
Preparation time **20 minutes,
plus soaking and chilling**

1 ¼ cups **blanched almonds**
1 ¼ cups **cashew nuts**
juice and grated zest of
  1 large **lemon**
⅓ cup **water**
4 teaspoons **maple syrup**
5 **pitted dates**
1 ¼ cups **raspberries**
mint leaves, to decorate

Put the almonds into a bowl, pour over enough water to cover, and let soak for at least 2 hours, or preferably overnight.

Put the cashews, lemon zest and juice, measured water, and 2 teaspoons maple syrup into a food processor or blender and blend together. Transfer to a small bowl, cover, and chill.

Drain the almonds, then put into a clean food processor with the dates and blend to a stiff paste, adding a little water, if necessary. Take a generous tablespoon of the dough and roll into a ball, then push the ball into a mini tart pan, pressing to line the edges. Repeat with the remaining dough to line 6 mini tart pans. Chill for 20 minutes.

Remove the tart shells from the pans by running a knife around the edges. Spoon some of the cashew filling into each tart, then top with the raspberries. Drizzle with the remaining maple syrup and serve decorated with mint leaves.

For raspberry, almond & mango crisp, put 1 cup chopped dried apricots and the grated zest and juice of 1 orange in a bowl and let soak for 1 hour. Put 1 large peeled, pitted, and chopped mango into a shallow ovenproof dish and pour the apricots and juice over it, then sprinkle with 1 ¼ cups raspberries. Sprinkle with ¾ cup ground almonds (almond meal), then pour in 2 tablespoons melted coconut oil. Bake in a preheated oven, at 400°F, for 15 minutes, until lightly golden. Divide among 6 bowls and serve immediately. **Calories per serving 206**

index

239

acknowledgments

Senior Commissioning Editor Eleanor Maxfield
Project Editor Clare Churly
Design and Art Direction Penny Stock
Special Photography William Shaw
Food Stylist Joy Skipper
Prop Stylist Kim Sullivan
Picture Library Manager Jennifer Veall
Production Controller Sarah Kramer

Special photography © Octopus Publishing Group
Limited/William Shaw. **Additional photography** © Octopus
Publishing Group/Will Heap 23, 33, 63, 97, 117, 139, 177,
187, 233; David Munns 41, 85, 103, 151, 159, 193, 197,
207, 219, 223; Sean Myers 125, 203; Lis Parsons 15, 45,
51, 55, 127, 161, 175, 191, 215, 229, 231; William Reavell
165; Craig Robertson 201; Gareth Sambidge 155; William
Shaw 13, 27, 57, 61, 71, 73, 75, 81, 89, 93, 107, 123, 131,
133, 137, 145, 167, 209, 213, 217, 225.